ISBN: 9781314487138

Published by:
HardPress Publishing
8345 NW 66TH ST #2561
MIAMI FL 33166-2626

Email: info@hardpress.net
Web: http://www.hardpress.net

Sacred Harp

ZHV

THE

SACRED HARP.

"Sweet Harp of Zion
With trembling hand I wake thy holy strain;
With trembling hand I sweep thy sacred chord,
That poured of old its music to the Lord."

FIRST AMERICAN

FROM THE

FIFTEENTH LONDON EDITION.

PHILADELPHIA:

HENRY F. ANNERS.

PRINTED BY KING & BAIRD.

PREFACE.

In offering to the Public a new and very much enlarged edition of the SACRED HARP, the Publisher has to return his most grateful acknowledgments for the very favourable reception given to this little compilation on its first appearance. Further selections have since been carefully gleaned from every recent publication of merit, on the subject of sacred poetry; and no exertion has been spared to render the Work still more deserving of the favour it has received.

To enter into a laboured defence of devotional poetry here, would be superfluous and out of place. Though the harp of the sweet singer of Israel hangs silent on the willow, and will not respond to the touch of less hallowed hands, Religion is yet acknowledged to be in its very nature, of all subjects, the one best suited to the exercise of high and pure poetical talent; and the specimens collected in this volume, will, it is hoped, evince that such talent has been here successfully exerted.

" To allay the perturbations of the mind, and to set the affections to a right tune; to celebrate, in glorious and lofty hymns, the throne and equipage of God's Almightiness, and what he suffers to be wrought with high providence in his church; to paint out and describe whatever in religion is holy and sublime, and, in virtue, amiable or grave;" this, in the words of Milton, is the gift and the office of poetry.

That amid the changes and chances of this mortal life, the pious affections of his readers may be kindled, and their minds raised to lofty and glowing conceptions of the glorious attributes of the Almighty, or soothed into

"The daylight dreams of pensive piety,"

by the little Work now presented to their notice, even as the harp of David calmed

the troubled spirit of Saul; and that their
hearts may be warmed with praise and
thanksgiving for the great and manifold
mercies of God, is the earnest prayer of the
Compiler.

Dublin, January, 1831.

CONTENTS.

CONTENTS.

CONTENTS.

CONTENTS.

CONTENTS.

THE

SACRED HARP.

GLORY TO GOD AND TO THE LAMB.

POLLOK.

Harp, lift thy voice on high!—shout angels,
    shout!
And loudest, ye redeemed!   Glory to God,
And to the Lamb who bought us with his
    blood,
From every kindred, nation, people, tongue;
And washed, and sanctified, and saved our
    souls;
And gave us robes of linen pure, and crowns
Of life, and made us kings and priests to God.
Shout back to ancient Time!   Sing loud, and
    wave
Your palms of triumph!   Sing, Where is
    thy sting,

B

O Death!—where is thy victory, O Grave!
Thanks be to God, eternal thanks, who gave
Us victory through Jesus Christ, our Lord.
Harp, lift thy voice on high!—shout, angels,
 shout!
And loudest, ye redeemed! Glory to God,
And to the Lamb, all glory and all praise,
All glory and all praise, at morn and even,
That come and go eternally, and find
Us happy still, and Thee for ever blest!
Glory to God and to the Lamb. Amen.
For ever, and for ever more. Amen.

CHRIST THE ROCK OF AGES.

TOPLADY.

Rock of ages, cleft for me,
Let me hide myself in Thee;
Let the water and the blood,
From thy riven side which flow'd,
Be of sin the double cure,
Cleanse me from its guilt and pow'r.

Not the labours of my hands
Can fulfil thy laws demands;
Could my zeal no respite know,
Could my tears for ever flow;
All for sin could not atone,
Thou must save, and thou alone.

Nothing in my hand I bring,
Simply to thy cross I cling;
Naked, come to thee for dress,
Helpless, look to thee for grace;
Foul I to the fountain fly,
Wash me, Saviour, or I die.

While I draw this fleeting breath,
While my eye-strings break in death;
When I soar to worlds unknown,
See Thee on thy judgment throne.
Rock of ages, cleft for me,
Let me hide myself in Thee!

GOOD TIDINGS OF GREAT JOY.

MONTGOMERY.

ANGELS, from the realms of glory,
  Wing your flight o'er all the earth,
Ye who sang creation's story,
  Now proclaim Messiah's birth;
Come and worship,
Worship Christ the new-born King.

Shepherds, in the field abiding,
  Watching o'er your flocks by night,
God with man is now residing,
  Yonder shines the Infant-light;
Come and worship,
Worship Christ the new-born King.

Sages, leave your contemplations,
  Brighter visions beam afar;
Seek the great Desire of nations;
  Ye have seen his natal star;
Come and worship,
Worship Christ the new-born King.

Saints before the altar bending,
  Watching long in hope and fear,
Suddenly the Lord, descending,
  In his temple shall appear ;
Come and worship,
Worship Christ the new-born King.

Sinners, wrung with true repentance,
  Doom'd for guilt to endless pains,
Justice now revokes the sentence,
  Mercy calls you—break your chains ;
Come and worship,
Worship Christ the new-born King.

HYMN OF THE HEBREW MAID.

SIR WALTER SCOTT.

WHEN Israel, of the Lord beloved,
  Out from the land of bondage came,
Her father's God before her moved,
  An awful guide in smoke and flame.

By day along the astonish'd lands
    The cloudy pillar glided slow;
By night, Arabia's crimson'd sands
    Return'd the fiery pillar's glow.

There rose the choral hymn of praise,
    And trump and timbrel answer'd keen;
And Zion's daughters pour'd their lays,
    With priests' and warriors' voice between.
No portents now our foes amaze,
    Forsaken Israel wanders lone;
Our fathers would not know Thy ways,
    And Thou hast left them to their own.

But present still, though now unseen,
    When brightly shines the prosperous day,
Be thoughts of Thee a cloudy screen,
    To temper the deceitful ray.
And oh! when stoops on Judah's path,
    In shade and storm the frequent night,
Be Thou, long-suffering, slow to wrath,
    A burning and a shining light!

Our harps we left by Babel's streams
   The tyrant's jest, the Gentiles' scorn;
No censer round our altar beams,
   And mute are timbrel, trump, and horn.
But Thou hast said, " The blood of goat,
   The flesh of rams, I will not prize ;
A contrite heart, an humble thought,
   Are mine accepted sacrifice."

LIGHT SHINING OUT OF DARKNESS.

COWPER.

God moves in a mysterious way,
   His wonders to perform ;
He plants his footsteps in the sea,
   And rides upon the storm.

Deep in unfathomable mines
   Of never-failing skill,
He treasures up his bright designs,
   And works his sovereign will.

Ye fearful saints, fresh courage take,
　The clouds ye so much dread
Are big with mercy, and shall break
　In blessings on your head.

Judge not the Lord by feeble sense,
　But trust him for his grace;
Behind a frowning providence
　He hides a smiling face.

His purposes will ripen fast,
　Unfolding every hour;
The bud may have a bitter taste,
　But sweet will be the flower.

Blind unbelief is sure to err,
　And scan his work in vain;
God is his own interpreter,
　And he will make it plain.

THE DYING CHRISTIAN TO HIS SOUL.

POPE.

VITAL spark of heavenly flame!
Quit, O quit, this mortal frame:
Trembling, hoping, lingering, flying,
O the pain, the bliss of dying!
Cease, fond nature, cease thy strife
And let me languish into life.

Hark, they whisper; angels say,
Sister spirit, come away!
What is this absorbs me quite!
Steals my senses, shuts my sight;
Drowns my spirits, draws my breath:
Tell me my soul, can this be death?

The world recedes; it disappears!
Heaven opens on my eyes!—my ears
   With sounds seraphic ring;
Lend, lend your wings!—I mount!—I fly!
O grave!—where is thy victory?
   O death!—where is thy sting?

VICTORY OVER DEATH AND THE WORLD.

MILAN.

I'm going to leave all my sadness,
  I'm going to change earth for Heaven;
There, there all is peace, all is gladness,
  There pureness and glory are given.
    Come quickly then, Jesus. Amen.

Friends, weep not in sorrow of spirit,
  But joy that my time here is o'er;
I go the good part to inherit,
  Where sorrow and sin are no more.

The shadows of evening are fleeing;
  Morn breaks from the City of light;
This moment day starts into being,
  Eternity bursts on my sight!

The first-born redeem'd from all trouble,
  (The Lamb that was slain, in the throng,)
Their ardour in praising redouble;
  Breaks not on the ear their new song!

I'm going to tell their great story,
  To share in their transports of praise ;
I'm going in garments of glory,
  My voice to unite with their lays.

Ye fetters corrupted then leave me ;
  Thou body of sin droop and die ;
Pains of earth cease ye ever to grieve me ;
  From you 'tis for ever I fly.
    Come quickly then, Jesus.   Amen.

ELEGY ON A BELOVED INFANT.
ANON.

FARE thee well, thou lovely stranger,
  Guardian angels take your charge,
Freed at onee from pain and danger,
  Happy spirit set at large.

Life's most bitter cup just tasting,
  Short thy passage to the tomb,
O'er the barrier swiftly hasting
  To thine everlasting home.

Death his victim still pursuing,
  Ever to his purpose true,
Soon her placid cheek bedewing,
  Robbed it of its rosy hue.

Sealed those eyes, so lately beaming
  Innocence and joy so mild,
Every look so full of meaning
  Seemed to endear the lovely child.

In the silent tomb we leave her
  Till the resurrection morn,
When her Saviour will receive her,
  And restore her lovely form.

Then, dear Lord, we hope to meet her
  In thy happy courts above,
There with heavenly joy to greet her,
  And resound redeeming Love!

THE MEEKNESS OF CHRIST.

MILMAN.

Thou wert born of woman! thou didst
  come
O Holiest! to this world of sin and gloom,
Not in thy dread omnipotent array;
And not by thunders strewed was thy tem-
  pestuous road ;
Nor indignation burnt before thee on thy way,
  But thee, a soft and naked child,
  Thy mother undefiled,
  In the rude manger laid to rest
  From off her virgin breast.

The heavens were not commanded to pre-
  pare
A gorgeous canopy of golden air :
Nor stoop'd their lamps th' enthroned fires
A single silent star came wandering from
  afar,
Gliding unchecked and calm along the liquid
  sky.

The eastern sages leading on
As at a kingly throne,
To lay their gold and odours sweet
Before thy infant feet.

The earth and ocean were not hushed to
    hear
Bright harmony from every starry sphere;
Nor at thy presence brake the voice of song
From all the cherub choirs; and seraph's
    burning lyres
Poured thro' the host of heaven the charmed
    host along.
        One angel troop the strain began,
        Of all the race of man
        By simple shepherds heard alone,
        That soft Hosannah's tone.

And when thou didst depart, no ear of
    flame
To bear thee hence in lambent radiance
    came :

Nor visible angels mourned with drooping
    plumes:
Nor didst thou mount on high from fatal
    Calvary
With all thine own redeemed outbursting
    from their tombs.

> For thou didst bear away from earth
> But one of human birth,
> The dying felon by thy side, to be
> In Paradise with thee.

Nor o'er thy cross the clouds of vengeance
    brake;
A little while the conscious earth did shake
At that foul deed by her fierce children
    done;
A few dim hours of day the world in dark-
    ness lay;
Then bask'd in bright repose beneath the
    cloudless sun.

> While thou didst sleep beneath the
>   tomb,
> Consenting to thy doom:

Ere yet the white-robed angel shone
Upon the sealed stone.

And when thou didst arise, thou didst not
    stand
With devastation in thy red right hand,
Plaguing the guilty city's murtherous
    crew;
But thou didst haste to meet thy mother's
    coming feet,
And bear the words of peace unto the
    faithful few.
      Then calmly, slowly didst thou rise
      Into the native skies,
      Thy human form dissolved on high
      In its own radiancy.

LOVE TO PARENTS.

NOEL.

To honour those who gave us birth,
To cheer their age, to feel their worth,
Is God's command to human kind,
And own'd by every grateful mind.

Trace then the tender scenes of old,
And all our infant days unfold ;
Yield back to sight the mother's breast,
Watchful to lull her child to rest.

Survey her toil, her anxious care,
To form the lisping lips to pray'r ;
To win for God the yielding soul,
And all its ardent thoughts controul.

Nor hold from mem'ry's glad review
The fears which all the father knew ;
The joy that mark'd his thankful gaze
As virtue crown'd maturer days.

C

When press'd by sickness, pain, or grief,
How anxious they to give relief!
Our dearest wish they held their own:
Till our's return'd, their peace was flown.

God of our life, each parent guard,
And death's sad hour, O long retard!
Be their's each joy that gilds the past,
And heaven our mutual home at last.

THE STAR OF BETHLEHEM.

KIRKE WHITE.

WHEN marshall'd on the nightly plain,
  The glitt'ring host bestud the sky;
One star alone of all the train,
  Can fix the sinner's wandering eye.

Hark! hark! to God the chorus breaks
  From every host, from every gem;
But one alone the Saviour speaks,
  It is the Star of Bethlehem.

Once on the raging seas I rode,
　The storm was loud, the night was dark,
The ocean yawn'd—and rudely blow'd
　The wind that toss'd my found'ring bark.

Deep horrors then my vitals froze,
　Death-struck—I ceas'd the tide to stem;
When suddenly a star arose,
　It was the Star of Bethlehem.

It was my guide, my light, my all;
　It bade my dark forebodings cease;
And thro' the storm and danger's thrall,
　It led me to the port of peace.

Now safely moor'd—my perils o'er,
　I'll sing, first in night's diadem,
For ever and for evermore,
　The Star!—the Star of Bethlehem!

THE HEAVENLY JERUSALEM.

RAFFLES.

HIGH in yonder realms of light,
  Far above these lower skies,
Fair and exquisitely bright,
  Heaven's unfading mansions rise :
Built of pure and massy gold,
  Strong and durable are they ;
Deck'd with gems of worth untold,
  Subjected to no decay !

Glad within these blest abodes,
  Dwell the raptur'd saints above,
Where no anxious care corrodes,
  Happy in Emmanuel's love !
Once, indeed, like us below,
  Pilgrims in this vale of tears,
Torturing pain, and heavy woe,
  Gloomy doubts, distressing fears :

These, alas! full well they knew,
　Sad companions of their way;
Oft on them the tempest blew,
　Through the long and cheerless day!
Oft their vileness they deplor'd,
　Wills perverse and hearts untrue,
Griev'd they could not love their Lord,
　Love him as they wished to do.

Oft the big unbidden tear,
　Stealing down the furrow'd cheek,
Told, in eloquence sincere,
　Tales of woe they could not speak:
But these days of weeping o'er,
　Past this scene of toil and pain,
They shall feel distress no more,
　Never, never, weep again!

'Mid the chorus of the skies,
　'Mid the angelic lyres above,
Hark! their songs melodious rise,
　Songs of praise to Jesus' love!

Happy spirits! ye are fled,
 Where no grief can entrance find;
Lull'd to rest the aching head,
 Sooth'd the anguish of the mind!

All is tranquil and serene,
 Calm and undisturb'd repose;
There no cloud can intervene,
 There no angry tempest blows!
Every tear is wiped away,
 Sighs no more shall heave the breast;
Night is lost in endless day—
 Sorrow—in eternal rest!

FIRST SUNDAY AFTER EPIPHANY.

HEBER.

By cool Siloam's shady rill
 How sweet the lily grows!
How sweet the breath beneath the hill
 Of Sharon's dewy rose!

Lo! such the child whose feet
  The paths of peace have trod;
Whose secret heart, with influence sweet,
  Is upward drawn to God!

By cool Siloam's shady rill
  The lily must decay;
The rose that blooms beneath the hill
  Must shortly fade away.

And soon, too soon, the wintry hour
  Of man's maturer age;
Will shake the soul with sorrow's power,
  And stormy passion's rage!

O Thou, whose infant feet were found
  Within Thy Father's shrine!
Whose years, with changeless virtue crown'd,
  Were all alike Divine.

Dependant on Thy bounteous breath,
  We seek thy grace alone,
In childhood, manhood, age, and death,
  To keep us still Thine own!

THE DAY OF WRATH.

SIR WALTER SCOTT.

THE day of wrath!—that dreadful day,
When heaven and earth shall pass away,
What power shall be the sinner's stay?
Whom shall he trust that dreadful day?

When shrivelling like a parched scroll,
The flaming heavens together roll;
When, louder yet, and yet more dread,
Swells the high trump that wakes the dead.

Oh, on that day, that wrathful day,
When man to judgment wakes from clay,
Be Thou, O Christ! the sinner's stay,
Though heaven and earth shall pass away!

THE NAME OF JESUS.

NEWTON.

How sweet the name of Jesus sounds
  In a believer's ear!
It soothes his sorrows, heals his wounds,
  And drives away his fear.

It makes the wounded spirit whole,
  And calms the troubled breast;
'Tis manna to the hungry soul,
  And to the weary rest.

Dear name!—the rock on which I build,
  My shield and hiding-place;
My never-failing treasury, filled
  With boundless stores of grace.

By thee my prayers acceptance gain
  Although with sin defiled,
Satan accuses me in vain,
  And I am owned a child.

Jesus, my Shepherd, Husband, Friend,
   My Prophet, Priest, and King;
My Lord, my life, my way, my end,
   Accept the praise I bring.

Weak is the effort of my heart,
   And cold my warmest thought;
But when I see thee as thou art,
   I'll praise thee as I ought.

Till then I would thy love proclaim
   With every fleeting breath;
And may the music of thy name
   Refresh my soul in death.

MISSIONARY HYMN.

HEBER.

From Greenland's icy mountains,
   From India's coral strand,
Where Afric's sunny fountains
   Roll down their golden sand;

From many an ancient river,
  From many a balmy plain,
They call us to deliver
  Their land from error's chain.

What though the spicy breezes
  Blow soft on Ceylon's isle,
Though every prospect pleases,
  And only man is vile;
In vain with lavish kindness,
  The gifts of God are strown,
The heathen, in his blindness,
  Bows down to wood and stone.

Shall we whose souls are lighted
  With wisdom from on high,
Shall we to man benighted
  The lamp of life deny?
Salvation! oh, salvation!
  The joyful sound proclaim,
Till each remotest nation
  Has learnt Messiah's name.

Waft, waft ye winds his story!
   And you, ye waters, roll;
Till like a sea of glory,
   It spreads from pole to pole!
Till o'er our ransom'd nature,
   The Lamb for sinners slain,
Redeemer, King, Creator,
   In bliss returns to reign.

THE PLACE OF REST.

ANON.

THERE is an hour of peaceful rest
   To mourning wanderers given;
There is a tear for souls distrest,
A balm for every wounded breast—
   'Tis found above—in heaven!

There is a soft, a downy bed,
   'Tis fair as breath of even;
A couch for weary mortals spread,
Where they may rest their aching head,
   And find repose in heaven!

There is a home for weeping souls,
  By sin and sorrow driven,
When tost on life's tempestuous shoals,
Where storms arise, and ocean rolls,
  And all is drear—but heaven!

There faith lifts up the tearful eye,
  The heart with anguish riven;
And views the tempest passing by,
The evening shadows quickly fly,
  And all serene in heaven!

There fragrant flowers immortal bloom,
  And joys supreme are given:
There rays divine disperse the gloom;
Beyond the confines of the tomb
  Appears the dawn of heaven!

HUMAN LIFE.

KELLY.

WHAT is life ?—'tis all a vapour ;
  Soon it vanishes away ;
Life is like a dying taper ;
  Oh, my soul, why wish to stay ?
Why not spread thy wings and fly
Straight to yonder world of joy ?

See that glory, how resplendent !
  Brighter far than fancy paints,
There, in majesty transcendent !
  Jesus reigns, the king of saints.
Spread thy wings, my soul, and fly
Straight to yonder world of joy.

Joyful crowds his throne surrounding,
  Sing with rapture of his love,
Through the heavens his praises sounding,
  Filling all the courts above.
Spread thy wings, my soul, and fly
Straight to yonder world of joy.

Go and share his people's glory ;
  Midst the ransomed crowd appear ;
Thine a joyful wondrous story :
  One that angels love to hear.
Spread thy wings, my soul, and fly,
Straight to yonder world of joy.

HYMN FOR WHITSUNDAY.

HEBER.

SPIRIT of Truth ! on this thy day,
  To thee for help we cry,
To guide us through the dreary way
  Of dark mortality !

We ask not, Lord ! thy cloven flame,
  Or tongues of various tone ;
But long thy praises to proclaim
  With fervour in our own.

We mourn not that prophetic skill
  Is found on earth no more ;
Enough for us to trace Thy will
  In Scripture's sacred lore.

We neither have nor seek the power
  Ill demons to control;
But Thou, in dark temptation's hour
  Shalt chase them from the soul.

No heavenly harpings soothe our ear,
  No mystic dreams we share;
Yet hope to feel Thy comfort near,
  And bless Thee in our prayer.

When tongues shall cease, and power decay,
  And knowledge empty prove,
Do Thou Thy trembling servants stay,
  With Faith, with Hope, with Love!

THE BURIAL ANTHEM.

MILMAN.

BROTHER, thou art gone before us,
  And thy saintly soul is flown
Where tears are wiped from every eye,
  And sorrow is unknown.

From the burthen of the flesh,
  And from care and fear released,
Where the wicked cease from troubling,
  And the weary are at rest.

The toilsome way thou'st travelled o'er,
  And borne the heavy load,
But Christ hath taught thy languid feet
  To reach his blest abode ;
Thou'rt sleeping now, like Lazarus
  Upon his Father's breast,
Where the wicked cease from troubling,
  And the weary are at rest.

Sin can never taint thee now,
  Nor doubt thy faith assail,
Nor thy meek trust in Jesus Christ,
  And the Holy Spirit fail :
And there thou'rt sure to meet the good,
  Whom on earth thou loved'st best,
Where the wicked cease from troubling,
  And the weary are at rest.
          D

" Earth to earth," and " dust to dust,"
  The solemn priest hath said,
So we lay the turf above thee now,
  And we seal thy narrow bed :
But thy spirit, brother, soars away
  Among the faithful blest,
Where the wicked cease from troubling
  And the weary are at rest.

THE BIBLE.

SIR WALTER SCOTT.

WITHIN this awful volume lies
The mystery of mysteries ;
Happiest they of human race
To whom their God has given grace
To read, to fear, to hope, to pray,
To lift the latch, to force the way ;
And better had they ne'er been born,
Than read to doubt, or read to scorn.

THE DAY OF JUDGMENT.

ANON.

Lo! He comes, with clouds descending,
  Once for favoured sinners slain,
Thousand, thousand, saints attending,
  Swell the triumphs of his train;
Hallelujah!
Jesus now shall ever reign!

Every eye shall now behold him,
  Clothed in awful majesty;
Those who set at naught and sold him,
  Pierced and nailed him to the tree,
Deeply wailing,
Shall the Great Messiah see!

Every island, sea, and mountain,
  Heaven and earth shall flee away;
All who hate him must, confounded,
  Hear the trump proclaim the day,
" Come to judgment!
Come to judgment! Come away!"

Now, redemption, long expected,
  See in solemn. pomp appear !
All his saints, by men rejected,
  Now shall meet him in the air !
Hallelujah !
See the day of God appear !

Answer thine own Bride and Spirit !
  Hasten, Lord, the general doom !
Promised glory to inherit,
  Take thy pining exiles home ;
All creation
Travails, groans, and bids thee come

Yea ! Amen ! Let all adore thee,
  High on thine exalted throne ;
Saviour ! take the power and glory,
  Claim the kingdom for thine own !
O come quickly !
Hallelujah ! Come, Lord, Come !

THE MISSIONARY'S DEATH.

ANON.

WEEP not for the saint that ascends
  To partake of the joys of the sky,
Weep not for the seraph which bends
  With the worshipping chorus on high.
Weep not for the spirit now crowned,
  With the garland to martyrdom given,
O weep not for him, he has found
  His reward and his refuge in heaven.

But weep for their sorrows, who stand
  And lament o'er the dead by his grave,—
Who sigh when they muse on the land
  Of their home, far away o'er the wave :—
Who sigh when they think that the strife,
  And the toil, and the perils before them,
Must fill up the moments of life,
  'Till the anguish of death shall come o'er
    them.

And weep for the nations that dwell
  Where the light of the truth never shone,
Where anthems of praise never swell,
  And the love of the Lamb is unknown.
O weep!—for the herald that came
  To proclaim in their dwelling the story
Of Jesus, and life through his name,
  Has been summoned away to his glory.

Weep not for the saint that ascends
  To partake of the joys of the sky;
Weep not for the seraph that bends
  With the worshipping chorus on high:
But weep for the mourners who stand
  By the grave of their brother in sadness;
And weep for the heathen whose land
  Still must wait for the day-spring of glad-
    ness.

THE HOUR OF PRAYER.

HEMANS.

CHILD, amidst the flowers at play,
While the red light fades away;
Mother with thine earnest eye,
Ever following silently;
Father, by the breeze of eve,
Called thy harvest work to leave:
Pray!—ere yet the dark hours be,
Lift the heart and bend the knee.

Traveller, in the stranger's land,
Far from thine own household band;
Mourner, haunted by the tone
Of a voice from this world gone;
Captive, in whose narrow cell
Sunshine hath not leave to dwell;
Sailor, on the darkening sea,
Lift the heart and bend the knee.

Warrior, that from battle won,
Breathest now at set of sun;
Woman, o'er the lowly slain,
Weeping on his burial plain;
Ye that triumph, ye that sigh,
Kindred by one holy tie;
Heaven's first star alike ye see—
Lift the heart and bend the knee.

LIFE, DEATH, AND JUDGMENT.

MONTGOMERY.

Few, few and evil are thy days,
   Man, of a woman born!
Peril and trouble haunt thy ways:
   Forth, like a flower at morn,
The tender infant springs to light,
   Youth blossoms to the breeze,
Age, withering age, is cropt ere night;
   Man, like a shadow, flees.

And dost Thou look on such a one?
  Will God to judgment call
A worm for what a worm hath done
  Against the Lord of all?
—As fail the waters from the deep,
  As summer-brooks run dry,
Man lieth down in dreamless sleep,
  His life is vanity.

Man lieth down, no more to wake,
  Till yonder arching sphere
Shall with a roll of thunder break,
  And Nature disappear.
O hide me till thy wrath be past,
  Thou who canst slay or save!
Hide me, where hope may anchor fast,
  In my Redeemer's grave.

CHRIST OUR EXAMPLE IN SUFFERING.

MONTGOMERY.

Go to dark Gethsemane,
　Ye that feel the tempter's power,
Your Redeemer's conflict see,
　Watch with him one bitter hour;
Turn not from his griefs away;
Learn of Jesus Christ to die.

Follow to the judgment hall,
　View the Lord of life arraigned;
O the wormwood and the gall!
　O the pangs his soul sustained!
Shun not suffering, shame, or loss,
Learn of him to bear the cross.

Calvary's mournful mountain climb;
　There, adoring at his feet,
Mark that miracle of time,
　God's own sacrifice complete:
" It is finished!"—hear the cry!
Learn of Jesus Christ to die.

Early hasten to the tomb,
   Where they laid his breathless clay,
All is solitude and gloom,
   Who hath taken his away?
Christ is risen! He meets our eyes!
Saviour, teach us so to rise.

ON THE DEATH OF AN AGED MINISTER.

MONTGOMERY.

SERVANT of God, well done!
   Rest from thy loved employ;
The battle fought, the victory won,
   Enter thy Master's joy.

The voice at midnight came,
   He started up to hear;
A mortal arrow pierced his frame,
   He fell—but felt no fear.

Tranquil amidst alarms,
   It found him on the field,
A veteran slumbering on his arms,
   Beneath his red-cross shield.

His sword was in his hand,
Still warm with recent fight,
Ready that moment, at command,
Through rock and steel to smite.

It was a two-edged blade,
Of heavenly temper keen;
And double were the wounds it made,
Where'er it glanced between.

'Twas death to sin,—'twas life
To all who mourn'd for sin;
It kindled, and it silenced strife,
Made war and peace within.

Oft with its fiery force
His arm had quell'd the foe;
And laid, resistless in his course
The alien armies low.

Bent on such glorious toils,
The world to him was loss,
Yet all his trophies, all his spoils,
He hung upon the cross.

At midnight came the cry,
"To meet thy God prepare!"
He woke—and caught his Captain's eye;
Then, strong in faith and prayer,

His spirit, with a bound,
Left its encumbering clay;
His tent, at sunrise, on the ground,
A darken'd ruin lay.

The pains of death are past,
Labour and sorrow cease;
And, life's long warfare closed at last,
His soul is found in peace.

Soldier of Christ, well done!
Praise be thy new employ;
And while eternal ages run,
Rest in thy Saviour's joy.

THE STAR OF THE EAST.

CAMPBELL.

THE world lay hush'd in slumber deep,
  And darkness veil'd the mind,
When rose upon their shadowy sleep,
  The star that saves mankind.

It dawns o'er Bethl'hem's holy shed,
  And scatt'ring at the sight,
Heaven's idol-host at once have fled
  Before that awful light.

Led by the solitary star,
  To glory's poor abode,
Lo! wond'ring wisdom from afar
  Brings incense to her God.

Humility, on Judah's hills,
  Watching her fleecy care,
Turns to an angel voice, that fills
  With love the midnight air.

Like voices thro' yon bursting cloud,
  Announce th' Almighty plan;
Hymning, in adoration loud,
  "Peace and good-will to man."

THE REDEEMED IN HEAVEN.

WESLEY.

LIFT up your eyes of faith, and see
  Saints and angels joined in one;
What a countless company
  Meet before yon dazzling throne!
Each before his Saviour stands,
  All in milk-white robes array'd
Palms they carry in their hands,
  Crowns of glory on their head.

Saints, begin the endless song,
  Cry aloud in heav'nly lays;
Glory doth to God belong;
  God, the glorious Saviour, praise:

All salvation from him came ;
 Him, who reigns enthron'd on high ;
Glory to the bleeding Lamb,
 Let the morning stars reply.

Angel-powers the throne surround,
 Next the saints in glory they ;
Lull'd with the transporting sound,
 They their silent homage pay :
Prostrate on their face before
 God and his Messiah fall ;
Then in hymns of praise adore,
 Shout the Lamb, who died for all.

Be it so, they all reply,
 Him let all our orders praise ;
Him that did for sinners die,
 Saviour of the favour'd race.
Render we our God his right,
 Glory, wisdom, thanks, and pow'r ;
Honour, majesty, and might ;
 Praise him, praise him evermore !

THE HEAVENLY TEMPLE.

LOGAN.

WHERE high the heavenly temple stands,
The house of God not made with hands,
A great High Priest our nature wears,
The guardian of mankind appears.

He who for men their surety stood,
And pour'd on earth his precious blood,
Pursues in heaven his mighty plan,
The Saviour and the friend of man.

Though now ascended up on high,
He bends on earth a brother's eye;
Partaker of the human name,
He knows the frailty of our frame.

Our fellow-suff'rer yet retains
A fellow-feeling of our pains,
And still remembers in the skies,
His tears, his agonies, and cries.

E

In ev'ry pang that rends the heart,
The Man of Sorrows had a part;
He sympathises with our grief,
And to the suff'rer sends relief.

With boldness, therefore, at the throne
Let us make all our sorrows known,
And ask the aids of heav'nly power
To help us in the evil hour.

THE NATIVITY.

CAMPBELL.

WHEN Jordan hush'd his waters still,
And silence slept on Zion hill;
When Bethlehem's shepherds through the
    night
Watch'd o'er their flocks by starry light;

Hark! from the midnight hills around,
A voice of more than mortal sound,
In distant hallelujahs stole,
Wild murm'ring o'er the raptur'd soul.

Then swift to every startled eye,
New streams of glory light the sky;
Heav'n bursts her azure gates to pour
Her spirits to the midnight hour.

On wheels of light, on wings of flame,
The glorious hosts of Zion came;
High heav'n with songs of triumph rung,
While thus they struck their harps and sung.

O Zion! lift thy raptur'd eye,
The long-expected hour is nigh;
The joys of nature rise again,
The Prince of Salem comes to reign.

See, Mercy from her golden urn
Pours a rich stream to them that mourn;
Behold, she binds, with tender care,
The bleeding bosom of despair.

He comes, to cheer the trembling heart,
Bids Satan and his host depart;
Again the day-star gilds the gloom,
Again the bow'rs of Eden bloom!

O Zion ! lift thy raptur'd eye,
The long-expected hour is nigh ;
The joys of nature rise again,
The Prince of Salem comes to reign.

GOD GLORIFIED IN ALL HIS WORKS.

ADDISON.

THE spacious firmament on high,
With all the blue etherial sky,
And spangled heavens, a shining frame,
Their great original proclaim.

Th' unwearied Sun, from day to day,
Does his Creator's praise display,
And publishes to every land
The work of an Almighty hand.

Soon as the evening shades prevail,
The Moon takes up the wondrous tale,
And nightly, to the listening Earth,
Repeats the story of her birth :

While all the stars that round her burn,
And all the planets in their turn,
Confirm the tidings as they roll,
And spread the truth from pole to pole.

What though in solemn silence all
Move round the dark terrestrial ball,
What though nor voice nor minstrel sound
Among their radiant orbs be found.

With saints and angels they rejoice,
And utter forth their glorious voice:
For ever singing as they shine,
" The hand that made us is Divine!"

THE SONG OF THE ANGELS AT BETHLEHEM.

CAWOOD.

HARK! what mean those holy voices,
 Sweetly sounding through the skies?
Lo! the angelic host rejoices;
 Heavenly hallelujahs rise.

Listen to the wondrous story,
    Which they chaunt in hymns of joy :
" Glory in the highest, glory !
    Glory be to God most high !

" Peace on earth, good-will from heaven,
    Reaching far as man is found ;
Souls redeem'd, and sins forgiven ;—
    Loud our golden harps shall sound.

" Christ is born, the Great Anointed,
    Heaven and earth his praises sing !
O receive whom God appointed,
    For your Prophet, Priest, and King !

" Hasten, mortals, to adore Him ;
    Learn his name, and taste his joy ;
Till in heaven ye sing before Him,
    Glory be to God most high !

" Let us learn the wondrous story
    Of our great Redeemer's birth ;
Spread the brightness of his glory.
    Till it cover all the earth."

THE SONG OF THE HUNDRED AND FORTY AND FOUR THOUSAND.

MONTGOMERY.

WHAT are these in bright array,
This innumerable throng,
Round the altar night and day,
Hymning one triumphant song?
"Worthy is the Lamb once slain,
Blessing, honour, glory, power,
Wisdom, riches, to obtain,
New dominion every hour."

These through fiery trials trod,
These from great affliction came;
Now before the throne of God,
Seal'd with his almighty name;
Clad in raiment pure and white
Victor-palms in every hand,
Through their dear Redeemer's might,
More than conquerors they stand.

Hunger, thirst, disease unknown,
On immortal fruits they feed;
Them, the Lamb amidst the throne,
Shall to living fountains lead:
Joy and gladness banish sighs,
Perfect love dispels all fears,
And for ever from their eyes,
God shall wipe away the tears.

PRAYER FOR THE HOLY SPIRIT.

ANON.

Come, Holy Spirit, calm my mind,
And fit me to approach my God;
Remove each vain, each worldly thought
And lead me to thy blest abode.

Hast thou imparted to my soul
A living spark of holy fire?
O kindle now the sacred flame,
Make me to burn with pure desire.

Impress upon my wandering heart
The love that Christ to sinners bore;
Then mourn the wounds my sins produc'd,
And my redeeming God adore.

A brighter faith and hope impart,
And let me now my Saviour see;
O soothe and cheer my burden'd heart,
And bid my spirit rest in Thee!

THE RAINBOW.

KNOX.

When the floods of the Deluge to ocean had
     roll'd,
  And the green-mantled hills re-appeared;
When the vallies unfolded their blossoms of
     gold,
And Noah, the patriarch, came forth from
     his hold,
  The voice of Jehovah was heard—
The voice of Jehovah brought tidings of bliss
To the world late entomb'd in the fearful
     abyss.

" The smoke of thine offering hath come up
　　　on high,
　　Thou father of nations to be !
And now I my rainbow shall set in the sky,
When tempests are dark to thy terrified eye,
　　That shall bring consolation to thee—
To thousands of thousands that after thee
　　tread
The regions of life to the realms of the
　　dead.

" It is for a sign that I never again
　　With waters shall cover the earth ;
And the birds in ,the arbours shall warble
　　their strain,
And the cattle shall browse on the nourishing
　　plain,
　　And give to their progeny birth ;
And die as they died by the curse that I
　　spoke,
When my cov'nant of old by thy father was
　　broke.

" And thou, Noah, thou art preserv'd for thy
    worth,
To re-people the desolate world ;
To the climes of the south, to the isles of
    the north,
To the east and the west, shall thy children
    go forth,
With the white flags of ocean unfurled—
To publish my praises throughout every land,
And the judgments of vengeance that come
    from my hand.

" And seed-time and harvest shall duly be
    given
To the hopes and the hands of mankind ;
And summer and winter, and morning and
    even,
And the dew-drops of earth, and the light-
    rays of heaven,
And the cloud, and the rain, and the wind,
While earth on her orbit is destined to run,
And give her green breast to the beams of
    the sun."

JACOB WRESTLING WITH THE ANGEL.

WESLEY.

Part the First.

COME, O Thou traveller unknown,
Whom still I hold, but cannot see
My company before is gone,
And I am left alone with Thee;
With Thee all night I mean to stay,
And wrestle till the break of day.

I need not tell Thee who I am;
My misery and sin declare:
Thyself hast called me by my name;
Look on thy hands, and read it there:
But who, I ask Thee, who art Thou?
Tell me Thy name, and tell me now.

In vain Thou strugglest to get free,
I never will unloose my hold;
Art Thou the Man that died for me?
The secret of thy love unfold:
Wrestling, I will not let Thee go,
Till I thy name, thy nature know.

Wilt Thou not yet to me reveal
Thy new, unutterable name?
Tell me, I still beseech Thee, tell?
To know it now, resolved I am:
Wrestling, I will not let Thee go,
Till I thy name, thy nature know.

What though my shrinking flesh complain,
And murmur to contend so long?
I rise superior to my pain:
When I am weak, then I am strong:
And when my all of strength shall fail,
I shall with the God-man prevail.

Part the Second.

YIELD to me now, for I am weak,
But confident in self-despair;
Speak to my heart, in blessings speak;
Be conquer'dly my instant prayer:
Speak, or Thou never hence shalt move,
And tell me if thy name be Love.

'Tis Love!—'tis Love! Thou diedst for
    me,
I hear thy whisper in my heart:
The morning breaks, the shadows flee;
PURE, UNIVERSAL LOVE, THOU ART
To me, to all, thy bowels move;
Thy nature and thy name is Love.

My prayer hath power with God; the grace
Unspeakable I now receive;
Through faith I see Thee face to face;
I see Thee face to face, and live;
In vain I have not wept and strove;
Thy nature and thy name is Love.

I know Thee, Saviour, who Thou art,
Jesus, the feeble sinner's friend:
Nor wilt Thou with the night depart,
But stay and love me to the end:
Thy mercies never shall remove;
Thy nature and thy name is Love.

The Sun of Righteousness on me
Hath rose, with healing on his wings;
Wither'd my nature's strength; from Thee
My soul its life and succour brings;
My help is all laid up above;
Thy nature and thy name is Love.

Contented now upon my thigh
I halt, till life's short journey end;
All helplessness, all weakness, I
On Thee alone for strength depend;
Nor have I power from Thee to move:
Thy nature and thy name is Love.

Lame as I am, I take the prey;
Hell, earth, and sin, with ease o'ercome;
I leap for joy, pursue my way,
And, as a bounding hart, fly home;
Through all eternity, to prove,
Thy nature and thy name is Love.

NIGHT.

NOEL.

WHEN restless on my bed I lie,
Still courting sleep, which still will fly,
Then shall reflection's brighter power
Illume the lone and midnight hour.

If hush'd the breeze, and calm the tide,
Soft will the stream of memory glide,
And all the past, a gentle train,
Waked by remembrance, live again.

Perhaps that anxious friend I trace,
Beloved till life's last throb shall cease,
Whose voice first taught a Saviour's worth,
A future bliss unknown on earth:

His faithful counsel, tender care,
Unwearied love, and humble prayer;—
Oh, these still claim the grateful tear,
And all my drooping courage cheer!

If loud the wind, the tempest high,
And darkness wraps the sullen sky,
I muse on life's tempestuous sea,
And sigh, O Lord, to come to Thee.

Toss'd on the deep and swelling wave,
Oh, mark my trembling soul, and save!
Give to my view that harbour near,
Where Thou wilt chase each grief and fear!

DIRGE OF RACHEL.

KNOX.

AND Rachel lies in Ephrath's land,
  Beneath her lonely oak of weeping;
With mouldering heart, and withering hand,
  The sleep of death for ever sleeping.

The spring comes smiling down the vale,
  The lilies and the roses bringing;
But Rachel never more shall hail
  The flowers that in the world are springing.

F

The Summer gives his radiant day
  And Jewish dames the dance are treading ;
But Rachel, on her couch of clay,
  Sleeps all unheeded and unheeding.

The Autumn's ripening sunbeam shines,
  And reapers to the field is calling ;
But Rachel's voice no longer joins
  The choral song at twilight's falling.

The Winter sends his drenching shower,
  And sweeps his howling blast around her ;
But earthly storms possess no power
  To break the slumber that hath bound
    her.

Thus round and round the Seasons go,
  But joy or grief no more betide her ;
For Rachel's bosom could not know
  Though friends were housed in death be-
    side her.

Yet time shall come, as prophets say,
  Whose dreams with glorious things are
    blended,
When Seasons on their changeful way
  Shall wend not as they long have wended.

Yes, time shall come, when flowers that
  bloom
Shall meet no storm their bloom to wither;
When friends, rejoicing from the tomb,
  Have gone to heavenly climes together.

THE SABBATH.

DODDRIDGE.

Lord of the Sabbath! hear us pray,
In this thy house, on this thy day;
Accept, as grateful sacrifice,
The songs which from thy temple rise.

Now met to pray, and bless thy name,
Whose mercies flow each day the same,
Whose kind compassions never cease ;
We seek instruction, pardon, peace.

Thine earthly Sabbaths, Lord! we love
But there's a nobler rest above :
Oh, that we might that rest attain
From sin, from sorrow, and from pain!

In thy bless'd kingdom we shall be
From every moral trouble free ;
No sighs shall mingle with the songs
Resounding from immortal tongues.

No rude alarms of raging foes,
No cares to break the long repose,
No midnight shade, no clouded sun,
But sacred, high, eternal noon.

O long-expected day, begin !
Dawn on this world of woe and sin :
Fain would we leave this weary road,
To sleep in death, and rest in God.

THE COMMUNION OF SAINTS.

MONTGOMERY.

Not to the mount that burn'd with fire,
To darkness, tempest, and the sound
Of trumpet waxing higher and higher,
Nor voice of words that rent the ground.
While Israel heard, with trembling awe,
Jehovah thunder forth his law:

But to Mount Zion we are come,
The city of the living God,
Jerusalem, our heavenly home,
The courts by angel-legions trod,
Where meet, in everlasting love,
The church of the first-born above:

To God, the Judge of quick and dead,
The perfect spirits of the just,
Jesus, our great new-covenant Head,
The blood of sprinkling,—from the dust,
That better things than Abel's cries,
And pleads a Saviour's sacrifice.

Oh, hearken to the healing voice,
That speaks from heaven in tones so mild !
To-day are life and death our choice ;
To-day, through mercy reconciled,
Our all to God we yet may give ;
   Now let us hear his voice and live.

DEATH EASY IN PROSPECT OF HEAVEN.

WATTS.

THERE is a land of pure delight,
  Where saints immortal reign,
Infinite day excludes the night,
  And pleasures banish pain.

There everlasting spring abides,
  And never-withering flowers :
Death, like a narrow sea, divides
  This heavenly land from ours.

Sweet fields, beyond the swelling flood,
   Stand dress'd in living green :
So to the Jews old Canaan stood,
   While Jordan roll'd between.

But timorous mortals start and shrink
   To cross this narrow sea,
And linger, shivering, on the brink,
   And fear to launch away.

Oh could we make our doubts remove,
   These gloomy doubts that rise,
And see the Canaan that we love,
   With unbeclouded eyes :

Could we but climb where Moses stood,
   And view the landscape o'er,
Not Jordan's stream, nor death's cold flood,
   Should fright us from the shore !

CHARACTER OF LORD BYRON.

POLLOK.

A MAN of rank, and of capacious soul,
Who riches had and fame, beyond desire,
An heir of flattery, to titles born,
And reputation, and luxurious life.
Yet, not content with ancestorial name,
Or to be known because his fathers were ;
He, on this height hereditary, stood,
And gazing higher, purposed in his heart
To take another step.   Above him seemed,
Alone, the mount of song, the lofty seat
Of canonized bards ; and thitherward,
By nature taught, and inward melody,
In prime of youth, he bent his eagle eye.
No cost was spared.   What books he wished
      he read ;
What sage to hear, he heard ; what scenes
      to see,
He saw.   And first, in rambling school-boy
      days,

Britannia's mountain-walks, and heath-girt
    lakes,
And story-telling glens, and founts, and
    brooks,
And maids, as dew-drops pure and fair, his
    soul
With grandeur filled, and melody and love.
Then travel came, and took him where he
    wished.
He cities saw, and courts, and princely
    pomp;
And mused alone on ancient mountain
    brows;
And mused on battle-fields, where valour
    fought
In other days; and mused on ruins gray,
With years; and drank from old and fabu-
    lous wells;
And plucked the vine that first-born prophets
    plucked;
And mused on famous tombs, and on the wave
Of Ocean mused, and on the desert waste.
The heavens and earth of every country saw.

Where'er the old inspiring Genii dwelt,
Aught that could rouse, expand, refine the
    soul,
Thither he went, and meditated there.
He touched his harp, and nations heard, en-
    tranced,
As some vast river of unfailing source,
Rapid, exhaustless, deep, his numbers flow-
    ed,
And oped new fountains in the human heart,
Where fancy halted, weary in her flight,
In other men, his, fresh as morning, rose,
And soared untrodden heights, and seemed
    at home,
Where angels bashful looked. Others,
    though great,
Beneath their argument seemed struggling
    whiles :
He, from above descending, stooped to touch
The loftiest thought ; and proudly stooped,
    as though
It scarce deserved his verse. With Nature's
    self,

He seemed an old acquaintance, free to jest
At will with all her glorious majesty.
He laid his hand upon "the Ocean's mane,"
And played familiar with his hoary locks.
Stood on the Alps, stood on the Appenines,
And with the thunder talked, as friend to
    friend ;
And wove his garland of the lightning's wing,
In sportive twist, the lightning's fiery wing,
Which, as the footsteps of the dreadful God,
Marching upon the storm in vengeance,
    seemed ;
Then turned, and with the grasshopper, who
    sung
His evening song beneath his feet, conversed.
Suns, moons, and stars, and clouds, his sis-
    ters were ;
Rocks, mountains, meteors, seas, and winds,
    and storms,
His brothers, younger brothers, whom he
    scarce
As equals deemed. All passions of all men,
The wild and tame, the gentle and severe ;

All thoughts, all maxims, sacred and pro-
    fane ;
All creeds, all seasons, time, eternity ;
All that was hated, and all that was dear ;
All that was hoped, all that was feared, by
    man,
He tossed about, as tempest-withered leaves,
Then, smiling, looked upon the wreck he
    made.
With terror now he froze the cowering blood,
And now dissolved the heart in tenderness ;
Yet would not tremble, would not weep
    himself ;
But back into his soul retired, alone,
Dark, sullen, proud, gazing contemptuously
On hearts and passions prostrate at his feet.
So Ocean, from the plains his waves had
    late
To desolation swept, retired in pride,
Exulting in the glory of his might,
And seemed to mock the ruin he had
    wrought.

Great man! the nations gazed, and wondered
    much,
And praised; and many called his evil good,
Wits wrote in favour of his wickedness;
And kings to do him honour took delight.
Thus, full of titles, flattery, honour, fame,
Beyond desire, beyond ambition, full,
He died. He died of what?—of wretched-
    ness.
Drank every cup of joy, heard every trump
Of fame, drank early, deeply drank, drank
    draughts,
That common millions might have quench-
    ed; then died
Of thirst, because there was no more to
    drink.
His goddess, Nature, wooed, embraced, en-
    joyed,
Fell from his arms abhorred; his passions
    died;
Died all but dreary solitary pride;
And all his sympathies in being, died.
As some ill-guided bark, well built and tall,

Which angry tides cast out on desert shore,
And then retiring, left it there to rot
And moulder in the winds and rains of
heaven;
So he, cut from the sympathies of life,
And cast ashore from Pleasure's boisterous
surge,
A wandering, weary, worn, and wretched
thing,
Scorched, and desolate, and blasted soul,
A gloomy wilderness of dying thought,—
Repined, and groaned, and withered from
the earth,
His groanings filled the land, his numbers
filled;
And yet he seemed ashamed to groan. Poor
man!
Ashamed to ask, and yet he needed help.
Proof this, beyond all lingering of doubt,
That not with natural or mental wealth,
Was God delighted, or his peace secured;
That not in natural or mental wealth;
Was human happiness or grandeur found.

Attempt how monstrous, and how surely
    vain !
With things of earthly sort, with aught but
    God,
With aught but moral excellence, truth, and
    love,
To satisfy and fill the immortal soul.
Attempt, vain inconceivably ! attempt,
To satisfy the Ocean with a drop,
To marry Immortality to Death,
And with the unsubstantial Shade of Time,
To fill the embrace of all Eternity !

A SUMMER EVENING.

WATTS.

How fine has the day been, how bright was
    the sun,
How lovely and joyful the course that he
    run,
Though he rose in a mist when his race he
    begun,
    And there follow'd some droppings of rain!

But now the fair traveller's come to the west,
IIis rays are all gold, and his beauties are
    best ;
IIe paints the sky gay as he sinks to his rest,
    And foretels a bright rising again.

Just such is the Christian ; his course he be-
    gins,
Like the sun in a mist, when he mourns for
    his sins
And melts into tears ; then he breaks out
    and shines,
    And travels his heavenly way :
But when he comes nearer to finish his race,
Like a fine setting sun, he looks richer in
    grace,
And gives a sure hope, at the end of his days,
    Of rising in brighter array.

THE EXEMPLARY WIFE.

KNOX.

O BLEST is he whose arms infold
  A consort virtuous as fair!
Her price is far above the gold
  That worldly spirits love to share.
On her, as on a beauteous isle,
  Amid life's dark and stormy sea,
In all his trouble, all his toil,
  He rests with deep security.

Even in the night-watch dark and lone,
  The distaff fills her busy hand;
Her husband in the gates is known
  Among the elders of the land;
Her household all delight to share
  The food and raiment she bestows,—
Even she with a parent's care
  Regards their weakness and their woes.

G

Her pitying hand supplies the poor,
 The widowed one, the orphan child
Like birds assembled round her door,
 When sweeps the winter tempest wild.
Her lips, with love and wisdom fraught,
 Drop, like the honey-comb, their sweets;
The young are by her dictates taught,
 The mourner her condolence meets.

Her lovely babes around her rise—
 Fair scions of a holy stem !
And deeply shall her bosom prize
 The blessings she receives from them.
Beauty is vain—the summer bloom
 To which a transient fate is given ;
But her's awaits a lasting doom
 In the eternal bowers of Heaven.

HYMN BEFORE THE SACRAMENT.

HEBER.

BREAD of the world, in mercy broken!
Wine of the soul, in mercy shed!
By whom the words of life were spoken,
And in whose death our sins are dead!

Look on the heart by sorrow broken,
Look on the tears by sinners shed,
And be Thy feast to us the token
That by Thy grace our souls are fed!

THE DEATH OF THE SCEPTIC AND CHRISTIAN.

R. MONTGOMERY.

—How will the sceptic brave the hour
Of death's divine, inexorable power,
When all this fairy world shall glide away,
Like midnight dreams before the morning
ray?

See! how he shudders at the thought of
    death;
What doubt and horror hang upon his breath;
The gibb'ring teeth, glaz'd eye, and marble
    limb,—
Shades from the tomb stalk out, and stare`
    on him!

Lo! there, in yonder fancy-haunted room,
What mutter'd curses trembled through the
    gloom,
When pale, and shiv'ring, and bedew'd with
    fear,
The dying sceptic felt his hour drew near;
From his parch'd tongue no sainted murmurs
    fell,
No bright hopes kindled at his faint farewell;
As the last throes of death convuls'd his cheek,
He gnash'd and scowl'd, and raised a hideous
    shriek;
Rounded his eyes into a ghastly glare;
Lock'd his white lips—and all was mute de-
    spair!

Go, child of darkness, see a Christian die,
No horror pales his lip, or rolls his eye ;
No dreadful doubts, or dreamy terrors, start
The hope Religion pillows on his heart.
When with a dying hand he waves adieu
To all who love so well, and weep so true ;
Meek, as an infant to the mother's breast
Turns fondly longing for its wonted rest,
He pants for where congenial spirits stray,
Turns to his God, and sighs his soul away.

THE LITTLE WANDERING JEW.

ANON.

Far, far from Zion, far from God,
And suffering still the chast'ning rod ;
Hopeless, and homeless, meets your view,
A little, weary, wand'ring Jew !

No Father's name, no worship sweet,
No Saviour's love, no mercy-seat—
Blessings his nation brought to you—
Now glad the little weary Jew !

O Christian Gentiles! can you hear
That gospel to your souls so dear;
And yet, no sympathy from you,
Await the little wand'ring Jew?

Or canst thou view the eastern star,
Which brought the wise men from afar,
And whilst it shines so bright on you,
Forget the darkness of the Jew!

Or canst thou hear thy God's address,
" Who blesseth thee, I'll ever bless;"
And yet refuse the tribute due,
To teach and cheer the little Jew!

THE PROMISED SAVIOUR.

CAMERON.

Hark! the glad sound, the Saviour comes,
The Saviour promis'd long;
Let ev'ry heart exult with joy,
And ev'ry voice be song!

On Him the Spirit, largely shed,
  Exerts its sacred fire;
Wisdom and might, and zeal and love,
  His holy breast inspire.

He comes!—the pris'ners to relieve,
  In Satan's bondage held;
The gates of brass before him burst,
  The iron fetters yield.

He comes!—from dark'ning scales of vice,
  To clear the inward sight;
And on the eye-balls of the blind
  To pour celestial light.

He comes!—the broken hearts to bind,
  The bleeding souls to cure;
And with the treasures of his grace
  T' enrich the humble poor.

The sacred year has now revolv'd,
  Accepted of the Lord;
When Heaven's high promise is fulfill'd,
  And Israel is restored.

Our glad hosannahs, Prince of Peace
    Thy welcome shall proclaim ;
And heaven's exalted arches ring
    With thy most honour'd name.

————

VERSES BY THE LATE PRINCESS AMELIA, DAUGHTER OF GEORGE III.

UNTHINKING, idle, wild, and young,
I laugh'd, and talk'd, and danc'd, and sung ;
And, proud of health, of freedom vain,
Dreamed not of sorrow, care, or pain,
Concluding in those hours of glee,
That all the world was made for me.

But when the days of trial came,
When sickness shook this trembling frame ;
When folly's gay pursuits were o'er,
And I could dance and sing no more,
It then occurred how sad 'twould be
Were this world only made for me.

PRAYER.

MONTGOMERY.

PRAYER is the soul's sincere desire,
　Unutter'd or exprest ;
The motion of a hidden fire,
　That trembles in the breast.

Prayer is the burden of a sigh,
　The falling of a tear ;
The upward glancing of an eye,
　When none but God is near.

Prayer is the simplest form of speech
　That infant lips can try ;
Prayer the sublimest strains that reach
　The Majesty on high.

Prayer is the Christian's vital breath,
　The Christian's native air ;
His watchword at the gates of death,
　He enters heaven by prayer.

Prayer is the contrite sinner's voice,
  Returning from his ways ;
While angels in their songs rejoice,
  And say, " Behold, he prays !"

The saints in prayer appear as one
  In word, and deed, and mind,
When with the Father and his Son
  Their fellowship they find.

Nor prayer is made on earth alone,
  The Holy Spirit pleads :
And Jesus on the eternal throne
  For sinners intercedes.

O Thou by whom we come to God,
  The life, the truth, the way,
The path of prayer Thyself hast trod
  Lord, teach us how to pray !

PRAISE FOR THE FOUNTAIN OPENED.

COWPER.

THERE is a fountain fill'd with blood,
   Drawn from Emmanuel's veins;
And sinners, plunged beneath that flood,
   Lose all their guilty stains.

The dying thief rejoiced to see
   That fountain in his day;
And there have I, as vile as he,
   Wash'd all my sins away.

Dear dying Lamb, thy precious blood
   Shall never lose its power,
Till all the ransom'd church of God
   Be saved to sin no more.

E'er since, by faith, I saw the stream
   Thy flowing wounds supply,
Redeeming love has been my theme,
   And shall be till I die.

Then in a nobler, sweeter song,
  I'll sing thy power to save;
When this poor lisping, stamm'ring tongue
  Lies silent in the grave.

Lord, I believe thou hast prepared
  (Unworthy though I be)
For me a blood-bought free reward,
  A golden harp for me !

'Tis strung, and tuned, for endless years,
  And formed by power divine ;
To sound in God the Father's ears
  No other name than thine.

MORNING HYMN.

BISHOP KENN.

Awake, my soul, and with the sun,
Thy daily stage of duty run ;
Shake off dull sloth, and joyful rise
To pay thy morning sacrifice.

Thy precious time mispent, redeem;
Each present day thy last esteem;
Improve thy talent with due care,
For the great day thyself prepare.

In conversation be sincere,
Keep conscience as the noon-tide clear,
Think how the all-seeing God, thy ways,
And all thy secret thoughts, surveys.
Wake, and lift up thyself, my heart,
And with the angels bear thy part;
Who all night long, unwearied sing
High praise to the eternal King.

Lord, I my vows to thee renew;
Scatter my sins as morning dew;
Guard my first springs of thought and will,
And with thyself my spirit fill.
Direct, control, suggest, this day,
All I design, or do, or say;
That all my powers, with all their might
In thy sole glory may unite.

EVENING HYMN.

BISHOP KENN.

GLORY to Thee, my God, this night,
For all the blessings of the light.
Keep me, O keep me, King of kings,
Under thy own almighty wings.
Forgive me, Lord, for thy dear Son,
The ill that I this day have done;
That with the world, myself, and Thee,
I, ere I sleep, at peace may be.

Teach me to live—that I may dread
The grave as little as my bed;
To die—that this vile body may
Rise glorious at the awful day.
O may my soul on Thee repose,
And may sweet sleep my eyelids close;
Sleep that may me more vigorous make,
To serve my God when I awake.

When in the night I sleepless lie,
My soul with heavenly thoughts supply ;
Let no ill dreams disturb my rest,
No powers of darkness me molest.
Praise God from whom all blessings flow ;
Praise Him all creatures here below ;
Praise Him above, ye heavenly host,
Praise Father, Son, and Holy Ghost.

SACRAMENTAL HYMN.

MORRISON.

'Twas on that night, when doom'd to know
The eager rage of every foe,
That night in which he was betray'd,
The Saviour of the world took bread :

And after thanks and glory given
To Him that rules in earth and heaven,
That symbol of his flesh he broke,
And thus to all his followers spoke :—

" My broken body thus I give,
For you, for all ; take, eat, and live ;
And oft the sacred rite renew,
That brings my wond'rous love to view.'

Then in his hands the cup he rais'd,
And God anew he thank'd and prais'd ;
While kindness in his bosom glow'd,
And from his lips salvation flow'd :

" My blood I thus pour forth," he cries,
" To cleanse the soul in sin that lies ;
In this the covenant is seal'd,
And Heaven's eternal grace reveal'd.

" With love to man this cup is fraught,
Let all partake the sacred draught ;
Through latest ages let it pour
In mem'ry of my dying hour."

THE HOUSE OF GOD.

EDMESTON.

There's a refuge of peace from the tempests
    that beat,
From the dark clouds that threaten, from the
    wild wind that blows :
A holy, a sweet, and a lovely retreat,
A spring of refreshment, a place of repose.

'Tis the house of my God—'tis the dwelling
    of prayer—
'Tis the temple all hallowed by blessing and
    praise ;
If sorrow and faithlessness conquer me there,
My heart to the throne of his grace I can
    raise.

For a refuge like this, ah ! what praises are
    due
For a rest so serene, for a covert so fair ;
Ah, why are the seasons of worship so few ?
Ah, why are so seldom the meetings of
    prayer ?

H

HYMN OF PRAISE.

WESLEY.

Source of being, source of light,
With unfading beauties bright;
Thee, when morning greets the skies,
Blushing sweet with humid eyes:
Thee, when soft declining day
Sinks in purple waves away;
Thee, O parent, will I sing,
To thy feet my tribute bring!

Yonder azure vault on high,
Yonder blue, low, liquid sky;
Earth on its firm basis placed,
And with circling waves embraced;
All creating pow'r confess,
All their mighty Maker bless;
Shaking nature with thy nod,
Earth and heaven confess their God.

Source of light, thou bidst the sun
On his burning axles run;
Stars like dust around him fly,
Strew the area of the sky;
Fills the queen of solemn night
From his vase her orb of light;
Lunar lustre, thus we see,
Solar virtue shines by thee.

Father, King, whose heav'nly face
Shines serene upon our race;
Mindful of thy guardian care,
Slow to punish, prone to spare;
We thy majesty adore,
We thy well-known aid implore;
Not in vain thy aid we call,
Nothing want, for thou art all!

THE FIELD OF GILBOA.

KNOX.

THE sun of the morning looked forth from
his throne,
And beamed on the face of the dead and
the dying,
For the yell of the strife like the thunder had
flown,
And red on Gilboa the carnage was lying.

And there lay the husband that lately was
pressed
To the beautiful cheek that was tearless
and ruddy;
But the claws of the eagle were fixed in his
breast,
And the beak of the vulture was busy and
bloody.

And there lay the son of the widowed and sad,
  Who yesterday went from her dwelling
    for ever;
Now the wolf of the hills a sweet carnival had
  On the delicate limb that had ceased not to
    quiver.

And then came the daughter, the delicate
    child,
  To hold up the head that was breathless
    and hoary;
And then came the maiden, all frantic and
    wild,
  To kiss the loved lips that were gasping
    and gory.

And then came the consort that struggled in
    vain
  To stem the red tide of a spouse that be-
    reft her;
And then came the mother that sunk 'mid
    the slain,
  To weep o'er the last human stay that
    was left her.

Oh, bloody Gilboa! a curse ever lie
  Where the king and his people were
    slaughter'd together:
May the dew and the rain leave thy herbage
  to die,
Thy flocks to decay, and thy forests to
  wither!

THE SISTER'S VOICE.

BROWNE.

Oh, my sister's voice is gone away;
  Around our social hearth
We have lost its tones, that were so gay
  So full of harmless mirth—
We miss the glancing of her eye,
  The waving of her hair,
The footsteps lightly gliding by,
  The hand so small and fair;
And the wild bright smile that lit her face,
  And made our hearts rejoice—
Sadly we mourn each vanished grace,
  But most of all her voice.

For, oh! it was so soft and sweet
  When breathed forth in words;
Such tones it had as hearts repeat
  In echoes on their chords;
And lovely when in measure soft
  She sung a mournful song,
And heavenly when it swelled aloft
  In triumph chorus strong;
And dearest when its words of love
  Would soothe our bosoms' care;
And loveliest when it rose above
  In sounds of praise and prayer.

Oh, in my childhood I have sate,
  When that sweet voice hath breathed,
Forgetful of each merry mate—
  Of the wild flowers I had wreathed:
And though each other voice I scorned
  That called me from my play,
If my sweet sister only warned,
  I never could delay.

'Twas she who sang me many a rhyme,
    And told me many a tale,
And many a legend of old time
    That made my spirit quail.

There are a thousand pleasant sounds
    Around our cottage still—
The torrent that before it bounds,
    The breeze upon the hill;
The murmuring of the wood-dove's sigh
    The swallow in the eaves;
And the wind that sweeps a melody
    In passing from the leaves;
And the pattering of the early rain,
    The opening flowers to wet—
But they want my sister's voice again,
    To make them sweeter yet.

We stood around her dying bed,
    We saw her blue eyes close;
While from her heart the pulses fled,
    And from her cheek the rose.

And still her lips in fondness moved,
  And still she strove to speak
To the mournful beings that she loved,
  And yet she was too weak :
Till at last from her eye came one bright ray,
  That bound us like a spell ;
And as her spirit passed away,
  We heard her sigh, '' Farewell !''

And oft since then that voice hath come
  Across my heart again ;
And it seems to speak as from the tomb,
  And bids me not complain :
And I never hear a low soft flute,
  Or the sound of a rippling stream,
Or the rich deep music of a lute,
  But it renews my dream,
And brings the hidden treasures forth
  That lie in memory's store ;
And again to thoughts of that voice gives
    birth—
  That voice I shall hear no more.

No more!—it is not so—my hope
  Shall still be strong in Heaven—
Still search around the spacious scope
  For peace and comfort given.
We know there is a world above,
  Where all the blessed meet,
Where we shall gaze on those we love,
  Around the Saviour's feet :
And I shall hear my sister's voice
  In holier, purer tone—
With all those spotless souls rejoice
  Before the Eternal Throne.

———

SATURDAY NIGHT.

WALKER.

AGAIN the week's dull labours close ;
The sons of toil from toil repose ;
And fast the evening gloom descends,
While home the weary peasant wends.

This night his eyes, in slumber sweet,
Shall droop their lids; to-morrow greet
A day of calm content and rest—
To Labour's aching limbs how blest!

Now, ere I seek my peaceful bed,
And on the pillow rest my head,
Oh, come, my soul, and wide display
The mercies of the week and day!
From danger who my frame hath kept,
While waking, and what time I slept?
Who hath my every want supplied,
And to my footsteps proved a guide?

Tis thou, my God!—to Thee belong
Incense of praise, and hallowed song;
To Thee be all the glory given,
Of all my mercies under heaven.
From Thee my daily bread and health,
Each comfort—all my spirit's wealth,
Have been derived; my sins alone,
And errings I can call my own.

Oh, when to-morrow's sun shall rise,
And light once more shall glad these eyes,
May I thy blessed Sabbath prove,
A day of holy rest and love.
May my Redeemer's praises claim
My constant thought ; the Spirit's flame
Descend, my accents to inspire,
And fill my soul with rapture's fire.

And when the night of Death is come,
And I must slumber in the tomb,
Oh, then, my God, this faint heart cheer,
And far dispel the shades of fear,
And teach me, in thy strength, to tread
The path which leads me to the dead,
Assured, when life's hard toils are o'er,
Of rest with Thee for evermore !

THE LILY.

TIGHE.

How withered, perished seems the form
  Of yon obscure, unsightly root!
Yet from the blight of wintry storm
  It hides secure the precious fruit.

The careless eye can find no grace,
  No beauty in the scaly folds;
Nor see within the dark embrace
  What latent loveliness it holds.

Yet in that bulb, those sapless scales,
  The lily wraps her silver vest;
Till vernal suns and vernal gales
  Shall kiss once more her fragrant breast.

Yes, hide beneath the mouldering heap,
  The undelighting, slighted thing;
There in the cold earth buried deep,
  In silence let it wait the spring.

Oh ! many a stormy night shall close
    In gloom upon the barren earth,
While still, in undisturbed repose,
    Uninjured lies the future birth ;

And Ignorance, with sceptic eye,
    Hope's patient smile shall wondering view
Or mock her fond credulity,
    As her soft tears the spot bedew.

Sweet smile of hope ! delicious tear !
    The sun, the shower indeed shall come ;
The promised verdant shoot appear,
    And nature bid her blossoms bloom.

And thou, O virgin queen of spring !
    Shalt, from thy dark and lowly bed,
Bursting thy green sheath's silken string,
    Unveil thy charms, and perfume shed.

Unfold thy robes of purest white,
    Unsullied from their darksome grave ;
And thy soft petals' silvery light,
    In the mild breeze unfettered wave.

So faith shall seek the lowly dust,
  Where humble sorrow loves to lie,
And bid her thus her hopes entrust,
  And watch with patient cheerful eye ;

And bear the long, cold, wintry night,
  And bear her own degraded doom,
And wait till Heaven's reviving light—
  Eternal Spring !—shall burst the gloom.

EVENING.

KEEBLE.

'Tis gone, that bright and orbed blaze,
Fast fading from our wistful gaze ;
Yon mantling cloud has hid from sight,
The last faint pulse of quivering light.

In darkness and in weariness
The traveller on his way must press,
No gleam to watch on tree or tower,
Whiling away the lonesome hour.

Sun of my soul! Thou Saviour dear,
It is not night if Thou be near:
Oh, may no earth-born cloud arise
To hide Thee from thy servant's eyes.

When round thy wondrous works below
My searching rapturous glance I throw,
Tracing out Wisdom, Power, and Love,
In earth or sky, in stream or grove:—

Or by the light thy words disclose
Watch Time's full river as it flows,
Scanning thy gracious Providence,
Where not too deep for mortal sense:—

When with dear friends sweet talk I hold,
And all the flowers of life unfold;—
Let not my heart within me burst,
Except in all I Thee discern.

When the soft dews of kindly sleep
My wearied eyelids gently steep,
Be my last thought, how sweet to rest
For ever on my Saviour's breast!

Abide with me from morn till eve,
For without Thee I cannot live:
Abide with me when night is nigh,
For without Thee I dare not die.

Thou Framer of the light and dark,
Steer through the tempest thine own ark;
Amid the howling wintry sea
We are in port if we have thee.

The rulers of this Christian land,
'Twixt Thee and us ordained to stand,—
Guide Thou their course, O Lord, aright,
Let all do all as in thy sight.

Oh, by thine own sad burthen, borne
So meekly up the hill of scorn,
Teach Thou thy Priests their daily cross
To bear as thine, nor count it loss!

If some poor wandering child of thine
Have spurn'd, to-day, the voice divine;
Now, Lord, the gracious work begin;
Let him no more lie down in sin.

I

Watch by the sick : enrich the poor
With blessings from thy boundless store :
Be every mourner's sleep to-night
Like infant's slumbers, pure and light.

Come near and bless us when we wake,
Ere through the world our way we take :
Till in the ocean of thy love,
We lose ourselves in heaven above.

STANZAS.

WALKER.

THOUGH under this monument sleep
    The relics of one who was dear ;
If living, her absence I'd weep,
    Her death shall occasion no tear.
If I loved—if I prized thee, my friend,
    My love shall now bid me rejoice,
And hope that I yet may ascend,
    Where angels list unto thy voice.

The sun shall no more be thy light,
  When thou walkest abroad in the day;
Nor the moon break the darkness of night,
  Where thy footsteps of purity stray;
For light now has found thee, that knows
  No change in its lustre or name;
Thy Saviour's own countenance throws
  Around thee this heavenly flame.

Thou never again shalt feel pain,
  Nor want, nor temptation, nor woe;
For He, on Mount Calvary slain,
  Hath finished thy grief's overthrow;
And this grave, upon which I recline,
  Holds nothing pertaining to thee,
But the frail and the mouldering shrine
  Of a soul, from corruption set free.

THE SAINT.

MARRIOTT.

A SAINT! oh, would that I could claim
The privileg'd, the honour'd name,
And confidently take my stand,
Though lowest in the saintly band.

Would, though it were in scorn applied,
That term the test of truth could bide!
Like kingly salutations given,
In mockery to the King of Heaven.

A saint! and what imports the name,
Thus banded in derision's game?
" Holy, and separate from sin ;
To good, nay even to God akin."

Is such the meaning of the name,
From which a Christian shrinks with shame?
Yes, dazzled by the glorious sight,
He owns his crown is all too bright.

And ill might son of Adam dare,
Alone such honour's weight to bear;
But fearlessly he takes the load,
United to the Son of God.

A saint! oh, scorner, give some sign,
Some seal to prove the title mine,
And warmer thanks thou shalt command,
Than bringing kingdoms in thy hand.

Oh! for an interest in that name,
When hell shall ope its jaws of flame
And sinners to their doom be hurl'd,
While scorned saints "shall judge the world."

How shall the name of saint be prized,
Tho' now neglected and despis'd,
When truth shall witness to the Lord,
That none but "saints shall judge the world."

THE SUFFERINGS OF CHRIST.

HARDY.

ALONE to the shade of Gethsemane's garden,
The Saviour repair'd when the Supper was
  o'er:
Weigh'd down with the load of their guilt
  for whose pardon
Such wonders of sorrow and suffering he
  bore:
As he sunk to the earth all mournful he
  cried,
"O Father! behold in compassion thy Son—
Now let this cup pass," then, as plaintive he
  sighed,
Exclaim'd, "Not my will, but thine, Father,
  be done."

Like blood-drops the sweat from his cold
  brow was streaming;
His bosom heav'd high with a tumult of woe,
From his eye, with the softest compassion
  still beaming,
The tears, like a torrent, incessantly flow:

With a ruffian band leagued, see the traitor
    appears,
"Hail, Master," exclaiming; betrays with a
    kiss;
They mock at his sorrows, nor pity his tears,
Oh, say, was there ever such sorrow as his?

Tho' guiltless, condemned, on the cross now
    behold him,
Suspended in agony: from his pierc'd side
See how the blood flows! while those who
    have sold him,
With taunts and reproaches his suff'rings
    deride:
Yet still his last breath for his murd'rers is
    spent,
"Oh, Father, forgive them!" in mercy, he
    cries;
Earth shakes to its centre—the temple is
    rent,
He exclaims, "It is finish'd," groans deeply,
    and dies.

ELIJAH'S INTERVIEW WITH GOD.

ANON.

On Horeb's rock the prophet stood,
  The Lord before him pass'd—
A hurricane in angry mood,
  Swept by him strong and fast:
The forests fell before its force,
The rocks were shivered by its course;
  God rode not in the blast—
'Twas but the whirlwind of his breath,
Announcing danger, wreck, and death.

It ceased—the air was mute—a cloud
  Came hiding up the sun,
When through the mountains deep and loud,
  An earthquake thundered on:
The frighted eagle sprang in air,
The wolf ran howling from his lair:
  God was not in the storm—
'Twas but the rolling of his car,
The trampling of his steeds from far.

'Twas still again, and nature stood,
  And calm'd her ruffled frame;
When swift from heaven a fiery flood,
  To earth devouring came:
Down to the depths the ocean fled,
The sick'ning sun look'd wan and dead,
  Yet God fill'd not the flame:
'Twas but the fierceness of his eye,
That lighted through the troubled sky.

At last a voice, all still and small,
  Rose sweetly on the ear,
Yet rose so clear and shrill, that all
  In heaven and earth might hear:
It spoke of peace, it spoke of love,
It spoke as angels speak above,
  And God himself was near!
For O! it was a Father's voice,
That bade his trembling world rejoice.

Speak, gracious Lord, speak ever thus,
  And let thy terrors prove
But harbingers of peace to us,
  But heralds of thy love!

Come through the earthquake, fire and storm,
Come in thy mildest, sweetest form,
  And all our fears remove;
One word from thee is all we claim—
Be that one word, a Saviour's name!

THE MILLENNIUM.

EDMESTON.

It seems, as if the summer sky
  Assumed a purer blue;
It seems, as if the flowret's dye
  Put on a brighter hue;
A loveliness, so soft, so fair,
Pervades the earth, the sea, and air;
Peace dwells below, and all above
Bespeaks the reign of heavenly Love.

Within the cot, within the tower,
  Wherever we may roam;
In city, field, or summer bower
  How sweet is every home!

Love and Religion, mingling there,
Make all alike around it fair :
Oh, this is love, surpassing far,
What all mere earthly passions are.

Such is the love that reigns around,
   In palace, hall, or cot,
The looks that beam, the words that sound,
   The joy that decks the spot:
The hymn floats softly through the vale,
The scent of flowers is in the gale,
Combining joy and summer sun,
Perfume, and music, all in one.

If heav'n has ever shone below
   Its dawning now appears ;
We seem to catch the morning glow,
   From those celestial spheres ;
This is the time so long foreseen,
When ages roll their years between ;
Oh, may it be an endless reign,
Nor earth know other rule again !

REFLECTIONS ON RETIRING TO REST.

BENTHAM.

It is good, when we lay on the pillow our
    head,
And the silence of night all around us is
    spread,
To reflect on the deeds we have done thro'
    the day,
Nor allow it to pass without profit away.

A day—what a trifle!—and yet the amount
Of the days we have pass'd form an awful
    account :
And the time may arrive when the world we
    would give,
Were it ours, might we have but another to
    live.

In whose service have we through the day
    been employ'd,
And what are the pleasures we mostly en-
    joyed ?

Our desires and our wishes to what did they
  tend—
To the world we are in, or the world without
  end ?

Hath the sense of his presence encompass'd
  us round,
Without whom not a sparrow can fall to the
  ground ?
Have our hearts turn'd to him with devotior
  most true,
Or been occupied only with things that we
  view ?

Have we often reflected how soon we must
  go
To the mansions of bliss, or the regions of
  woe ?
Have we felt unto God a repentance sincere,
And in faith to the Saviour of sinners drawn
  near ?

Let us thus with ourselves solemn conference
    hold,
Ere sleep's silken fetters our senses enfold;
And forgiveness implore for the sins of the
    day,
Nor allow them to pass unrepented away.

CHRISTIAN WARFARE.

CHARLOTTE ELIZABETH.

Soldier, go—but not to claim
    Mouldering spoils of earth-born treasure,
Not to build a vaunting name,
    Not to dwell in tents of pleasure.
Dream not that the way is smooth,
    Hope not that the thorns are roses;
Turn no wishful eye of youth,
    Where the sunny beam reposes;
      Thou hast sterner work to do,
      Hosts to cut thy passage through:
Close behind thee gulfs are burning—
Forward!—there is no returning.

Soldier, rest—but not for thee
  Spreads the world her downy pillow;
On the rock thy couch must be,
  While around thee chafes the billow:
Thine must be a watchful sleep,
  Wearier than another's waking;
Such a charge as thou dost keep
  Brooks no moment of forsaking.
    Sleep, as on the battle-field,
    Girded—grasping sword and shield:
Those thou canst not name or number,
Steal upon thy broken slumber.

Soldier, rise—the war is done:
  Lo, the hosts of hell are flying,
'Twas thy Lord the battle won;
  Jesus vanquished them by dying.
Pass the stream—before thee lies
  All the conquered land of glory;
Hark!—what songs of rapture rise,
  These proclaim the victor's story,

Soldier, lay thy weapons down,
Quit the sword, and take the crown;
Triumph! all thy foes are banished,
Death is slain, and earth has vanished.

ISAIAH'S VISION.

COOPER.

High on a throne of burnish'd gold,
With rays of Godhead crown'd,
Jehovah sat; his thunders roll'd,
And glory sparkled round.

His flowing train, of glittering white,
The spacious temple fill'd;
The angels, dazzled at the sight,
With wings their faces veil'd.

Around the throne, in burning row,
The six-wing'd seraphs stood;
While millions, flying to and fro,
Tun'd all their harps to God.

"Thrice holy, holy Lord," they cry,
" The God of Sabaoth thou;
Thy glory fills the worlds on high,
And fills the world below."

DEATH OF A YOUNG CHRISTIAN.
ANON.

O GRIEVE not for him with the wildness of
sorrow,
As those who in hopeless despondency
weep:
From God's holy word consolation we bor-
row,
For souls who in Jesus confidingly sleep.

Lament not your lov'd one, but triumph the
rather
To think of the promise, the pray'r of the
Lamb;
"Your joy shall be full," and "I will, oh,
my Father!
That those whom thou giv'st me may be
where I am."

K

Nay, weep not for him—for the flower of the
morning
So dear to your bosom, so fair in your eyes;
But weep for the souls unbelievingly scorn-
ing
The counsel and truth of the " God only
wise."

He came to the cross when his young cheek
was blooming,
And rais'd to the Lord the bright beam of
his eye;
And when o'er its beauty death's darkness
was glooming,
The cross did uphold him, the Saviour was
nigh,

I saw the black pall o'er his relics extended,
I wept, but they were not the tear-drops
of woe:
The pray'r of my soul that in fervour ascended,
Was, " Lord, when thou callest, like him
may I go!"

TRUST IN GOD.

COWPER.

God of my life, to thee I call,
Afflicted at thy feet I fall,
When the great water-floods prevail,
Leave not my trembling heart to fail.

Friend of the friendless and the faint!
Where shall I lodge my deep complaint?
Where but with thee, whose open door
Invites the helpless and the poor!

Did ever mourner plead with thee,
And thou refuse that mourner's plea?
Does not the word still fix'd remain,
That none shall seek thy face in vain?

That were a grief I could not bear,
Didst thou not hear and answer pray'r;
But a prayer-hearing, answ'ring God,
Supports me under ev'ry load.

Fair is the lot that's cast for me;
I have an advocate with thee:
They whom the world caresses most,
Have no such privilege to boast.

Poor tho' I am, despised, forgot,
Yet God, my God, forgets me not;
And he is safe, and must succeed,
For whom the Lord vouchsafes to plead.

THE LAND WHICH NO MORTAL MAY KNOW.

BARTON.

THOUGH earth has full many a beautiful
   spot,
  As a poet or painter might show;
Yet more lovely and beautiful, holy and
   bright,
To the hopes of the heart, and the spirit's
   glad sight,
  Is the land which no mortal may know.

There the crystalline stream, bursting forth
    from the throne.
  Flows on, and for ever will flow;
Its waves, as they roll, are with melody rife,
And its waters are sparkling, with beauty
    and life,
  In the land which no mortal may know.

Oh! who but must pine, in this dark vale of
    tears
  From its clouds and its shadows to go,
To walk in the light of the glory above,
And to share in the peace, and the joy, and
    the love
  Of the land which no mortal may know!

FEMALE CHARITY.

BARRET.

Woman all exceeds
In ardent sanctitude and pious deeds,
And chief in Woman charities prevail
That soothe when sorrows or disease assail.

As dropping balm medicinal instils
Health when we pine, her tears alleviate ills;
And the moist emblems of her pity flow
As heav'n relented with the wat'ry bow.
Let pearls embellish tresses, dew the morn,
But beauties more divine the maid adorn,
When mourning him she loved, her tender
      tear,
That else had blest his bed, imbathes his
      bier.

Ask the poor pilgrim on this convex cast,
His grizzled locks distorted in the blast;
Ask him what accent soothes, what hand
      bestows
The cordial bev'rage, garment, and repose;
Oh, he will dart a spark of ancient flame,
And clasp his tremulous hands, and Woman
      name!
Peruse the sacred volume, Him who died
Her kiss betray'd not, nor her tongue denied.
While even the apostle left him to his doom,
She linger'd round his cross and watched his
      tomb.

THE MORNING STAR.

ANON.

STAR of the morn, whose placid ray
  Beam'd mildly o'er yon sacred hill,
While whisp'ring zephyrs seem'd to say,
  As silence slept, and earth was still,
Hail, harbinger of gospel light?
Dispel the shades of nature's night!

I saw thee rise on Salem's towers,
  I saw thee shine on gospel lands,
And Gabriel summon'd all his powers
  And wak'd to ecstacy his bands;
Sweet cherubs hail'd thy rising ray,
And sang the dawn of gospel day!

Shine, lovely star, on every clime,
  For bright thy peerless beauties be;
Gild with thy beam the wing of time,
  And shed thy rays from sea to sea;
Then shall the world from darkness rise,
Millennial glories cheer our eyes!

HYMN FOR THE SONS OF THE CLERGY.

MRS. GRANT.

How blest those olive plants that grow
    Beneath the altar's sacred shade,
Where streams of fresh instruction flow,
    And Comfort's humble board is spread.

'Twas thus the swallow rear'd her young,
    Secure within the house of God,
Of whom the royal prophet sung,
    When banish'd from that blest abode.

When, like the swallow's tender brood,
    They leave the kind paternal dome,
On weary wing to seek their food,
    Or find in other climes a home ;

Where'er they roam, where'er they rest,
    Through all the varied scenes of life,
Whether with tranquil plenty blest,
    Or doom'd to share the deadly strife ;

Still may the streams of grace divine
  Glide softly near their devious way;
And faith's fair light serenely shine,
  To change their darkness into day.

Still may they with fraternal love
  Each other's shield and aid become;
And while through distant realms they rove,
  Remember still their childhood's home;

The simple life, the frugal fare,
  The kind parental counsels given,
The tender love, the pious care,
  That early winged their hopes to heaven.

And when the evening shades decline,
  And when life's toilsome task is o'er,
May they each earthly wish resign,
  And holier, happier climes explore.

And when the faithful shepherds view
  Each ransom'd flock around them spread,
How will they bless the plants that grew
  Beneath the altar's sacred shade!

"IT IS FINISHED."

BLAIR.

BEHOLD the Saviour on the cross,
 A spectacle of woe!
See from his agonizing wounds
 The blood incessant flow;

Till death's pale ensigns o'er his cheek
 And trembling lips were spread;
Till light forsook his closing eyes,
 And life his drooping head!

'Tis finished—was his latest voice;
 These sacred accents o'er,
He bow'd his head, gave up the ghost,
 And suffered pain no more.

'Tis finish'd—the Messiah dies
 For sins, but not his own;
The great redemption is complete,
 And Satan's power o'erthrown.

'Tis finish'd—all his groans are past ;
  His blood, his pains, and toils,
Have fully vanquished our foes,
  And crown'd him with their spoils.

'Tis finish'd—legal worship ends,
  And gospel ages run ;
All old things now are past away,
  And a new world begun.

THE LITANY.

GRANT.

SAVIOUR ! when in dust to thee,
Low we bow th' adoring knee,
When, repentant, to the skies
Scarce we lift our streaming eyes,—
Oh, by all the pains and woe,
Suffered once for man below,
Bending from thy throne on high,
Hear our solemn litany !

By thy helpless infant years,
By thy life of wants and tears,
By thy days of sore distress,
In the savage wilderness,—
By the dread permitted hour
Of th' insulting tempter's power,—
Turn, O turn a pitying eye,
Hear our solemn litany !

By the sacred griefs that wept,
O'er the grave where Lazarus slept,
By the boding tears that flowed
Over Salem's loved abode,—
By the anguished tear that told
Treachery lurked within thy fold,—
From thy seat above the sky,
Hear our solemn litany !

By thine hour of dire despair,
By thine agony of prayer,
By the cross, the nail, the thorn,
Piercing spear, and torturing scorn,

By the gloom that veiled the skies
O'er the dreadful sacrifice,
Listen to our humble cry,
Hear our solemn litany!

By the deep expiring groan,
By the sad sepulchral stone,
By the vault whose dark abode
Held in vain the rising God,—
Oh, from earth to heaven restored,
Mighty re-ascended Lord,
Listen, listen to the cry
Of our solemn litany!

THE CROSS OF CHRIST.

BOWRING.

In the Cross of Christ I glory!—
    Towering o'er the wrecks of time,
All the light of sacred story
    Gathers round its head sublime.

When the woes of life o'ertake me,
  Hopes deceive and fears annoy,
Never shall the cross forsake me,
  Lo! it glows with peace and joy!

When the sun of bliss is beaming
  Light and love upon my way,
From the cross the radiance streaming
  Adds more lustre to the day.

Bane and blessing, pain and pleasure,
  By the cross are sanctified;
Peace is there that knows no measure,
  Joys that through all time abide.

In the Cross of Christ I glory!—
  Towering o'er the wrecks of time,
All the light of sacred story
  Gathers round its head sublime.

THE WILD GAZELLE.

BYRON.

THE wild gazelle on Judah's hills
   Exulting yet may bound,
And drink from all the living rills
   That gush on holy ground;
Its airy step and glorious eye
May glance in tameless transport by :—

A step as fleet, an eye more bright,
   Hath Judah witness'd there;
And o'er her scenes of lost delight
   Inhabitants more fair.
The cedars wave on Lebanon,
But Judah's statelier maids are gone!

More blest each palm that shades those plains
   Than Israel's scattered race;
For, taking root, it there remains
   In solitary grace:
It cannot quit its place of birth,
It will not live in other earth.

But we must wander witheringly,
  In other lands to die ;
And where our father's ashes be,
  Our own may never lie :
Our temple hath not left a stone,
And Mockery sits on Salem's throne.

TO THE BUTTERFLY.

ROGERS.

CHILD of the sun ! pursue thy rapturous
    flight,
Mingling with her thou lov'st in fields of
    light :
And, where the flowers of Paradise unfold,
Quaff fragrant nectar from their cups of gold.
There shall thy wings, rich as an evening
    sky,
Expand and shut with silent ecstacy !

—Yet wert thou once a worm, a thing that
    crept
On the bare earth, then wrought a tomb and
    slept.
And such is man; soon from his cell of
    clay
To burst a seraph in the blaze of day!

THE RAINBOW.

CAMPBELL.

TRIUMPHAL arch, that fill'st the sky
    When storms prepare to part,
1 ask not proud philosophy
    To teach me what thou art.

Still seem as to my childhood's sight,
    A midway station given,
For happy spirits to alight
    Betwixt the earth and heaven.

L

Can all that optics teach, unfold
  Thy form to please me so,
As when I dreamt of gems and gold
  Hid in thy radiant bow ?

When science from creation's face
  Enchantment's veil withdraws,
What lovely visions yield their place
  To cold material laws ?

And yet, fair bow, no fabling dreams,
  But words of the Most High,
Have told why first thy robe of beams
  Was woven in the sky.

When o'er the green undeluged earth
  Heaven's covenant thou didst shine,
How came the world's grey fathers forth
  To watch thy sacred sign ?

And when its yellow lustre smil'd,
  Oe'r mountains yet untrod,
Each mother held aloft her child,
  To bless the bow of God.

Methinks thy jubilee to keep
  The first-made anthem rang,
On earth delivered from the deep,
  And the first poet sang.

How glorious is thy girdle cast
  O'er mountain, tower, and town,
Or mirror'd in the ocean vast,
  A thousand fathoms down.

As fresh in yon horizon dark,
  As young thy beauties seem,
As when the eagle from the ark
  First sported in thy beam.

For, faithful to its sacred page,
  Heaven still rebuilds thy span,
Nor lets the type grow pale with age,
  That first spoke peace to man.

THE RIGHTEOUS BLESSED IN DEATH.

MRS. BARBAULD.

How bless'd the righteous when he dies!
  When sinks a weary soul to rest,
How mildly beam the closing eyes,
  How gently heaves the expiring breast!

So fades a summer-cloud away,
  So sinks the gale when storms are o'er,
So gently shuts the eye of day,
  So dies a wave along the shore.

A holy quiet reigns around,
  A calm which life nor death destroys;
Nothing disturbs that peace profound,
  Which his unfettered soul enjoys.

Farewell, conflicting hopes and fears,
  Where lights and shades alternate dwell!
How bright the unchanging morn appears!
  Farewell, inconstant world, farewell'

Life's duty done, as sinks the clay,
    Light from its load the spirit flies;
While heaven and earth combine to say,
    "How bless'd the righteous when he dies!"

THE BEAUTIES OF CREATION.

HEBER.

I PRAISED the earth, in beauty seen,
With garlands gay of various green:
I praised the sea, whose ample field
Shone glorious as a silver shield:
And earth and ocean seemed to say,
" Our beauties are but for a day !"

I praised the sun, whose chariot rolled
On wheels of amber and of gold;
I praised the moon, whose softer eye
Gleamed sweetly through the summer sky !
And moon and sun in answer said,
" Our days of light are numbered !"

O God! O good beyond compare!
If thus thy meaner works are fair,
If thus thy bounties gild the span
Of ruined earth and sinful man,
How glorious must the mansion be,
Where thy redeemed shall dwell with thee!

THE SABBATH.

CUNNINGHAM.

DEAR is the hallowed morn to me,
  When village bells awake the day;
And, by their sacred minstrelsy,
  Call me from earthly cares away.

And dear to me the winged hour,
  Spent in thy hallowed courts, O Lord!
To feel devotion's soothing power,
  And catch the manna of thy word.

And dear to me the loud Amen,
  Which echoes through the blest abode,
Which swells and sinks, and swells again,
  Dies on the walls, but lives to God.

In secret I have often prayed,
  And still the anxious tear would fall;
But on thy sacred altar laid,
  The fire descends, and dries them all.

Oft when the world, with iron hands,
  Has bound me in his six-days' chain,
This bursts them, like the strong man's bands,
  And lets my spirit loose again.

Then dear to me the Sabbath morn,
  The village bells, the shepherd's voice;
These oft have found my heart forlorn,
  And always bid that heart rejoice.

Go, man of pleasure, strike thy lyre,
  Of broken Sabbath's sing the charms,
Ours be the prophet's car of fire,
  That bears us to a Father's arms.

THE DYING INFANT.

CECIL.

" CEASE here longer to detain me,
  Fondest mother, drowned in woe;
Now thy kind caresses pain me,
  Morn advances—let me go.

" See yon orient streak appearing!
  Harbinger of endless day;
Hark! a voice, the darkness cheering,
  Calls my new-born soul away!

" Lately launched, a trembling stranger,
  On the world's wild boisterous flood;
Pierced with sorrows, tossed with danger,
  Gladly I return to God.

" Now my cries shall cease to grieve thee,
  Now my trembling heart find rest;
Kinder arms than thine receive me,
  Softer pillow than thy breast.

" Weep not o'er these eyes that languish,
  Upward turning toward their home:
Raptured they'll forget all anguish,
  While they wait to see thee come.

" There, my mother, pleasures centre—
  Weeping, parting, care, or wo,
Ne'er our Father's house shall enter—
  Morn advances—let me go.

" As through this calm, this holy dawning,
  Silent glides my parting breath,
To an everlasting morning,
  Gently close my eyes in death.

" Blessings endless, richest blessings,
  Pour their streams upon thine heart,
(Though no language yet possessing,)
  Breathes my spirit ere we part.

" Yet to leave thee sorrowing rends me,
  Though again His voice I hear:
Rise! may every grace attend thee:
  Rise! and seek to meet me there."

THE VALUE OF A MOMENT.

MONTGOMERY.

At every motion of our breath,
Life trembles on the brink of death,
A taper's flame that upward turns,
While downward to the dust it burns.

A moment ushered us to birth,
Heirs of the commonwealth of earth,
Moment by moment, years are past,
And one ere long will be our last.

'Twixt that, long fled, which gave us light,
And that which soon shall end in night,
There is a point no eye can see,
Yet on it hangs eternity.

This is that moment,—who shall tell
Whether it leads to heaven or hell?
This is that moment,—as we choose,
The immortal soul we save or lose.

Time past and time to come are not,
Time present is our only lot;
O God, henceforth our hearts incline
To seek no other love than thine!

THE BETTER LAND.

HEMANS.

I HEAR thee speak of the better land,
Thou call'st its children a happy band;
Mother! oh, where is that radiant shore,—
Shall we not seek it and weep no more?
Is it where the flower of the orange blows,
And the fire-flies dance through the myrtle
     boughs?
"Not there, not there, my child."

Is it where the feathery palm-trees rise,
And the date grows ripe under sunny skies,
Or 'midst the green islands of glittering seas,
Where fragrant forests perfume the breeze,

And strange bright birds, on their starry
    wings,
Bear the rich hues of all glorious things?
  " Not there, not there, my child."

Is it far away in some region old,
Where the rivers wander o'er sands of gold—
Where the burning rays of the ruby shine,
And the diamond lights up the secret mine,
And the pearl gleams forth from the coral
    strand—
Is it there, sweet mother, that better land ?
  " Not there, not there, my child.

Eye hath not seen it, my gentle boy !
Ear hath not heard its deep songs of joy,
Dreams cannot picture a world so fair,
Sorrow and death may not enter there;
Time doth not breathe on its fadeless bloom,
For beyond the clouds, and beyond the tomb,
  It is there, it is there, my child !''

SEPARATION OF FRIENDS.

MONTGOMERY.

FRIEND after friend departs;
  Who hath not lost a friend?
There is no union here of hearts,
  That finds not here an end!
Were this frail world our final rest,
Living or dying none were blest.

Beyond the flight of time,—
  Beyond the reign of death,—
There surely is some blessed clime
  Where life is not a breath;
Nor life's affections transient fire,
Whose sparks fly upwards and expire.

There is a world above,
  Where parting is unknown:
A long eternity of love,
  Form'd for the good alone:
And faith beholds the dying here
Translated to that glorious sphere.

Thus star by star declines,
  Till all are past away :
As morning high and higher shines
  To pure and perfect day :
Nor sink those stars in empty night,
But hide themselves in heaven's own light.

SAUL JOURNEYING TO DAMASCUS.

ROSCOE.

Whose is that sword—that voice, and eye of
    flame,
That heart of unextinguishable ire ?
Who bears the dungeon-keys, and bonds,
    and fire ?
Along his dark and withering path he came,
Death in his looks, and terror in his name,
Tempting the might of heaven's Eternal
    Sire,
Lo ! the Light shone ! the sun's veiled
    beams expire—

A Saviour's self, a Saviour's lips proclaim !
Whose is yon form, stretched on the earth's
    cold bed,
With smitten soul and tears of agony
Mourning the past? Bowed is the lofty head,
Rayless the orbs that flashed with victory.
Over the raging waves of human will
The Saviour's spirit walked—and all was
    still !

MARY AT THE SEPULCHRE.

CUNNINGHAM.

How sweet, in the musing of faith, to repair
    To the garden where Mary delighted to
      rove ;
To sit by the tomb where she breathed her
    fond prayer,
    And paid her sad tribute of sorrow and
      love ;

To see the bright beam which disperses her
    fear,
  As the Lord of her soul breaks the bars of
    his prison,
And the voice of the angel salutes her glad
    ear,—
  The Lord is a captive no more—" He is
    risen !"

O Saviour! as oft as our footsteps we bend
  In penitent sadness to weep at thy grave,
On the wings of thy greatness in pity de-
    scend,
  Be ready to comfort and " mighty to
    save,"
We shrink not from scenes of desertion and
    wo,
  If there we may meet with the Lord of our
    love ;
Contented, with Mary, to sorrow below,
  If, with her, we may drink of thy foun-
    tains above.

SABBATH EVENING.

EDMESTON.

ANOTHER day has pass'd along,
  And we are nearer to the tomb?
Nearer to join the heavenly song,
  Or hear the last eternal doom.

These moments of departing day,
  When thought is calm, and labours cease,
Are surely solemn times to pray,
  To ask for pardon and for peace.

Thou God of mercy, swift to hear,
  More swift than man to tell his need;
Be THOU to us this evening near,
  And to thy fount our spirits lead.

Teach us to pray—and, having taught,
  Grant us the blessings that we crave;
Without thy teaching—prayer is nought
  But with it—powerful to save '
                M

Sweet is the light of Sabbath Eve,
  And soft the sunbeam lingering there,
Those sacred hours this low earth leave,
  Wafted on wings of praise and prayer.

This time, how lovely and how still !
  Peace shines, and smiles on all below;
The plain, the stream, the wood, the hill,
  All fair with evening's setting glow !

Season of Rest ! the tranquil soul
  Feels thy sweet calm, and melts in love:
And while these sacred moments roll,
  FAITH sees a smiling heaven above.

How short the time, how soon the sun
  Sets ! and dark night resumes her reign !
And soon the hours of rest are done,
  Then morrow brings the world again.

Yet will our journey not be long,
  Our pilgrimage will soon be trod ;
And we shall join the ceaseless song,
  The endless Sabbath of our GOD.

JESUS TEACHING THE PEOPLE.

BOWRING.

How sweetly flow'd the gospel's sound
  From lips of gentleness and grace,
When list'ning thousands gather'd round
  And joy and reverence fill'd the place.

From heaven he came—of heaven he spoke,
  To heaven he led his followers' way;
Dark clouds of gloomy night he broke,
  Unveiling an immortal day.

" Come, wanderers, to my Father's home,
  " Come, all ye weary ones, and rest !"
Yes ! sacred Teacher,—we will come—
  Obey thee,—love thee, and be blest '

Decay, then, tenements of dust !
  Pillars of earthly pride, decay !
A nobler mansion waits the just,
  And Jesus has prepared the way.

THE SCHEME OF REDEMPTION.

WATTS.

THE mighty frame of glorious grace,
That brightest monument of praise,
That e'er the God of love design'd,
Employs and fills my labouring mind.

Begin my soul the heav'nly song,—
A burden for an angel's tongue;
When Gabriel sounds these awful things
He tunes and summons all his strings.

Proclaim inimitable love!—
Jesus, the Lord of worlds above,
Puts off the beams of bright array,
And veils the God in mortal clay.

He that distributes crowns and thorns
Hangs on a tree, and bleeds and groans;
The Prince of Life resigns his breath;
The King of Glory bows to death!

But see the wonders of his power,—
He triumphs in his dying hour!
And while by Satan's rage he fell,
He dash'd the rising hopes of hell.

Thus were the hosts of death subdued
And sin aton'd by Jesus' blood:
Then he arose, and reigns above,
To conquer sinners by his love.

Who shall fulfil this boundless song!
The theme surmounts an angel's tongue:
How low, how vain, are mortal airs,
When Gabriel's nobler harp despairs!

THE THREE MOUNTAINS.

MONTGOMERY.

When on Sinai's top I see
God descend in majesty,
To proclaim his holy law,
All my spirit sinks with awe.

When in ecstacy sublime,
Tabor's glorious steep I climb,
At the too transporting light,
Darkness rushes o'er my sight.

When on Calvary I rest,
God, in flesh made manifest,
Shines in my Redeemer's face
Full of beauty, truth, and grace.

Here I would for ever stay,
Weep, and gaze my soul away;
Thou art heav'n on earth to me,
Lovely, mournful Calvary!

CHRISTIAN WATCHFULNESS.

CUNNINGHAM.

The God of Israel never sleeps;
The angelic band strict vigil keeps:
Above, below, amidst, around,
They float in air, or walk the ground;
Leave their bright mansion in the sky,
And watch the world with sleepless eye.

And, shall I then, the slave of sense,
Sink on the lap of indolence?
Shall I not wake, and watch, and pray,
Ere morn leads on the drowsy day;
And midst the shades of night prolong
'The patient prayer, and cheerful song!

Come, thou Great Shepherd of the sheep!
Come, Thou whose mercies never sleep!
Descend, as in the showers of spring;
Shed holy vigour from thy wing;
Thou swift to hear, and strong to bless,
Inspire the grace of " watchfulness!"

MOUNT CALVARY.

CUNNINGHAM.

FROM Calvary a cry was heard.
   A long reiterated cry:
My Saviour! every mournful word
   Bespeaks thy soul's deep agony.

A horror of deep darkness fell
  On thee, the Immaculate, the Just;
The congregated hosts of hell
  Combined to shake thy filial trust.

The scourge, the thorns, the deep disgrace,
  These thou could'st bear, and not repine;
But when JEHOVAH veiled his face,
  Unutterable pangs were thine.

Let the dumb world her silence break;
  Let pealing anthems rend the sky;
Awake, my sluggish soul, awake!
  He died, that we may never die!

Lord, on thy cross I fix my eye;
  If e'er I slight its pure control,
O let that dying, piercing cry
  Melt and reclaim my wandering soul!

KEDRON.

M. DE PLEURY.

THOU soft-flowing Kedron! by thy limpid
    stream
Our Saviour, at night, when the moon's sil-
    ver beam
Shone bright on thy waters, would often-
    times stray,
And lose in their murmrus the toils of the
    day;
Come, saints, and adore him, come, bow at
    his feet;
Oh! give him the glory, the praise that is
    meet!
Let joyful hosannas unceasing arise,
And join the full chorus that gladdens the
    skies!

How damp were the vapours that fell on his
    head!
How hard was his pillow! how humble his
    bed!

The angels beholding, amaz'd at the sight,
Attended their master with solemn delight :
Come, saints, and adore him, come bow at
 his feet
Oh ! give him the glory, the praise that is
 meet !
Let joyful hosannas unceasing arise,
And join the full chorus that gladdens the
 skies !

Oh, garden of Olivet ! dear, honour'd spot !
The fame of thy wonders shall ne'er be for-
 got !
The theme most transporting to seraphs
 above,
The triumph of sorrow, the triumph of love !
Come, saints, and adore him, come, bow at
 his feet :
Oh ! give him the glory, the praise that is
 meet !
Let joyful hosannas unceasing arise,
And join the full chorus that gladdens the
 skies !

THE ZION THAT IS ABOVE.

KELLY.

O Zion ! when I think of thee,
  I long for pinions like the dove ;
And mourn to think that I should be
  So distant from the land I love.

A captive exile far from home,
  For Zion's sacred walls I sigh,
With ransomed kindred there to come,
  And see Messiah eye to eye.

While here I walk on hostile ground,
  The few that I can call my friends
Are, like myself, in fetters bound,
  And weariness our steps attends.

But yet we hope to see the day,
  When Zion's children shall return ;
When all our griefs shall flee away,
  And we no more again shall mourn.

The thought that such a day will come,
　　Makes e'en the exile's portion sweet:
Though now we wander far from home,
　　In Zion soon we all shall meet.

TRUE AND FALSE GAIETY.

COWPER.

WHOM call we gay? That honour has long
　　been
The boast of mere pretenders to the name.
The innocent are gay—the lark is gay,
That dries his feathers, saturate with dew,
Beneath the rosy cloud, while yet the beams
Of dayspring overshoot his humble nest.
The peasant too, a witness of his song,
Himself a songster, is as gay as he.
But save me from the gaiety of those
Whose headachs nail them to a noonday
　　bed;

And save me too from theirs, whose haggard
    eyes
Flash desperation, and betray their pangs,
For property stripp'd off by cruel chance :
From gaiety, that fills the bones with pain,
The mouth with blasphemy, the heart with
    wo!

THE COMET.

CONDER.

Mysterious visitant! whose beauteous light
    Among the wondering stars so strangely
      gleams
Like a proud banner in the train of night,
    The unblazoned flag of Deity it streams ;
    Infinity is written in thy beams ;
And thought in vain would thro' the pathless
    sky
    Explore thy secret course ; thy circle seems
Too vast for time to grasp ;—O can that eye
Which numbers hosts like thee, this atom
    earth descry ?

O Thou, my every hope, my only fear;
Father of Lights, round whom the systems
 roll,
With all their suns and comets, sphere on
 sphere,
 Thy all-pervading energy, the soul,
 Thyself the centre of the mighty whole!
When death shall purge the film of sense
 away,
 And truth, with irresistible control,
Shall seize my ravish'd mind,—that awful
 day,
How shall my soul sustain that infinite sur-
 vey!

Then shall I shudder at the guilty past,
 And feel thy awful presence on my heart;
Was it at thee, oh, GOD, my sins I cast?
 Oh! on my trembling soul thy mercy dart,
 For now I feel how terrible thou art!
Thou wert All-present, and I saw thee not;
 Thou art my bliss, and yet I said, "De-
 part;"

Murmured, tho' boundless mercy fix'd my
    lot :—
And wilt thou own the soul that thee so oft
    forgot ?

Oh, wondrous thought ! the high and holy
    One
    Inhabiting eternity, will make
The humble soul his dwelling-place ; the sun
    Whose rising beams on orbs innumerous
      break,
    Does shine as much for the poor reptile's
      sake :
To Him is nothing great—is nothing small ;
    He fills a world,—he bids the insect take
His being full of bliss ;—He form'd them all ;
He guides the comet's course,—He marks
    the sparrow's fall.

Man—man, tho' in the dust his insect-birth,
    Beholds his nature unto GOD allied,
Link'd to the golden throne this creature earth
By ties that shall eternally abide :

Let suns, let systems perish—Jesus died
Nor shall one vital spark be quench'd in
    night,
  Which God has kindled:—Here my soul
    confide,
Safe in the arms of everlasting Might,
And circled with the beams of uncreated
    light.

THE HUNDREDTH PSALM.

ANON.

All people that on earth do dwell,
  Sing to the Lord with cheerful voice,
Him serve with mirth, his praise forth tell,
  Come ye before him and rejoice.
Know that the Lord is God indeed;
  Without our aid he did us make:
We are his flock, he doth us feed,
  And for his sheep he doth us take.

O enter then his gates with praise,
  Approach with joy his courts unto:
Praise, laud, and bless his name always,
  For it is seemly so to do.
For why? the Lord our God is good,
  His mercy is for ever sure;
His truth at all times firmly stood,
  And shall from age to age endure.

WALKING WITH GOD

COWPER.

OH! for a closer walk with God,
  A calm and heavenly frame;
A light, to shine upon the road
  That leads me to the Lamb!

Where is the blessedness I knew
  When first I saw the Lord?
Where is the soul-refreshing view
  Of Jesus, and his word?

N

What peaceful hours I once enjoyed !
How sweet their mem'ry still !
But they have left an aching void
The world can never fill.

Return, O holy Dove, return,
Sweet messenger of rest ;
I hate the sins that made thee mourn,
And drove thee from my breast.

The dearest idol I have known,
Whate'er that idol be,
Help me to tear it from thy throne,
And worship only thee.

So shall my walk be close with God,
Calm and serene my frame :
So purer light shall mark the road,
That leads me to the Lamb.

HAPPINESS.

TOPLADY.

HAPPINESS, thou lovely name,
  Where's thy seat, O tell me, where ?
Learning, pleasure, wealth, and fame,
  All cry out,—' It is not here :'
Not the wisdom of the wise
Can inform me where it lies;
Not the grandeur of the great
Can the bliss I seek create.

Object of my first desire,
  Jesus, crucified for me !
All to happiness aspire,
  Only to be found in thee :
Thee to praise, and thee to know,
Constitute our bliss below;
Thee to see, and thee to love,
Constitute our bliss above.

Lord, it is not life to live,
  If thy presence thou deny ;
Lord, if thou thy presence give,
  'Tis no longer death to die :
Source and giver of repose,
Singly from thy smile it flows ;
Peace and happiness are thine,
Mine they are, if thou art mine.

THE PASSION.

FROM THE OLD SPANISH.

EARTH and Heaven bewailing,
The light at mid-day failing,
The sea that sparkled cheerily
Rolling dark waves drearily ;
It was an hour of dread
When the Saviour said
Eli ! Eli ! from the tree,
Lord, I yield my soul to thee !

It was an hour of grieving
To angel and to man;
A quick convulsive heaving
Through nature's bosom ran:
Jehovah the great maker!
Of human pangs partaker!
The God that gave us breath,
For us to die the death!
It is a thought for gazing eyes,
But not for words, nor tears, nor sighs,
　　Jesus' dying agonies!

Mary, Mother, humbly kneeling,
I a smile of radiance stealing,
A holy smile! I see it break
A moonbeam o'er thy pallid cheek,
Oh! who may utter, who may think
What joy is mingled with my fears,
While Golgotha's dry dust doth drink
　　Jesus' blood and Mary's tears!

HEAVEN.

BOWLES.

Oh, talk to me of heaven; I love
To hear about my home above;
For there doth many a loved one dwell,
In light and joy ineffable.
Oh! tell me how they shine and sing,
While every harp rings echoing;
And every glad and tearless eye
Beams like the bright sun gloriously:
Tell me of that victorious palm
   Each hand in glory beareth;
Tell me of that celestial calm
   Each face in glory weareth.

Oh, happy, happy country! where
   There entereth not a sin;
And death who keeps its portals fair,
   May never once come in.
No grief can change their day to night;
The darkness of that land is light.

Sorrow and sighing God hath sent
Far thence to endless banishment.
And never more may one dark tear
  Bedim their burning eyes,
For every one they shed while nere,
  In fearful agonies,
Glitters a bright and dazzling gem
In their immortal diadem.

Oh, lovely, blooming country! there
Flourishes all that we deem fair.
And tho' no fields nor forests green
Nor bowery gardens there are seen,
  Nor perfumes load the breeze,
Nor hears the ear material sound,
Yet joys at God's right hand are found,
  The archetypes of these;
There is the home, the land of birth
Of all we highest prize on earth.
The storms that rack this world beneath
  Must there for ever cease;
The only air the blessed breathe
  Is purity and peace.

Oh, happy, happy land! in thee
Shines th' unveiled Divinity,
Shedding thro' each adoring breast
A holy calm, a halcyon rest.
And those blest souls whom death did sever,
Have met to mingle joys for ever.
Oh! soon may heaven unclose to me!
Oh! may I soon that glory see!
And my faint, weary spirit stand
Within that happy, happy land!

EMMAUS.

RAFFLES.

ABIDE with us—the evening shades
  Begin already to prevail;
And as the ling'ring twilight fades,
  Dark clouds along th' horizon sail.

Abide with us—the night is chill;
  And damp and cheerless is the air:
Be our companion, Stranger still,
  And thy repose shall be our care.

Abide with us—thy converse sweet
  Has well beguil'd the tedious way;
With such a friend we joy to meet,
  We supplicate thy longer stay.

Abide with us—for well we know
  Thy skill to cheer the gloomy hour,
Like balm thy honied accents flow,
  Our wounded spirits feel their pow'r.

Abide with us—and still unfold
  Thy sacred, thy prophetic lore;
What wondrous things of Jesus told!
  Stranger, we thirst, we pant for more.

Abide with us—and still converse
  Of him who late on Calv'ry died,
Of him the prophecies rehearse,
  He was our friend they crucified.

Abide with us—our hearts are cold,
  We thought that Israel he'd restore;
But sweet the truths thy lips have told,
  And, Stranger, we complain no more.

Abide with us—we feel the charm,
 That binds us to our unknown friend:
Here pass the night secure from harm,
 Here, Stranger, let thy wand'rings end.

Abide with us:—to their request
 The Stranger bows, with smiles divine;
Then round the board the unknown guesı
 And weary travellers recline.

Abide with us—amaz'd they cry,
 As suddenly, whilst breaking bread,
Their own lost Jesus meets their eye,
 With radiant glory on his head!

Abide with us—thou heavenly Friend,
 Leave not thy followers thus alone:
The sweet communion here must end,—
 The heav'nly visitant is gone!

THE SABBATH.

EAST.

Lord of the Sabbath and its light;
    I hail thy hallow'd day of rest;
It is my weary soul's delight,
    The solace of my care-worn breast.

Its dewy morn—its glowing noon—
    Its tranquil eve—its solemn night—
Pass sweetly; but they pass too soon,
    And leave me sadden'd at their flight.

Yet sweetly as they glide along,
    And hallow'd tho' the calm they yield;
Transporting tho' their rapt'rous song.
    And heav'nly visions seem reveal'd:

My soul is desolate and drear,
    My silent harp untun'd remains;
Unless, my Saviour, thou art near,
    To heal my wounds and soothe my pains.

O ever, ever let me hail
  Thy presence with thy day of rest!
Then will thy servant never fail
  To deem thy Sabbaths doubly blest.

THE REST OF THE GRAVE.

LOGAN.

How still and peaceful is the grave!
  Where, life's vain tumults past,
Th' appointed house, by Heav'n's decree,
  Receives us all at last.

The wicked there from troubling cease,
  Their passions rage no more;
And there the weary pilgrim rests
  From all the toils he bore.

There rest the pris'ners, now releas'd
  From slav'ry's sad abode;
No more they hear th' oppressor's voice,
  Or dread the tyrant's rod.

There, servants, masters, small and great,
  Partake the same repose ;
And there, in peace, the ashes mix
  Of those who once were foes.

All, levell'd by the hand of Death,
  Lie sleeping in the tomb ;
Till God in judgment calls them forth,
  To meet their final doom.

A SABBATH MEDITATION.

LEYDEN.

WITH silent awe I hail the sacred morn,
  That slowly wakes while all the fields are
    still ;
A soothing calm on every breeze is borne,
  A graver murmur gurgles from the rill,
  And echo answers softer from the hill,
And softer sings the linnet from the thorn ;
  The skylark warbles in a tone less shrill.

Hail, light serene ! hall, sacred Sabbath
 morn !
The rooks float silently, in airy drove ;
The sun a placid yellow lustre throws ;
 The gales, that lately sighed along the
 grove,
Have hushed their downy wings in dead re-
 pose ;
 The hovering rack of clouds forgets to
 move :—
So smiled the day when the first morn arose.

THE GOODNESS OF GOD.

BOWRING.

THE stars have sunk in yon concave blue,
And the sun is peeping through the dew ;
Thy Spirit, Lord ! doth nature fill—
Before thee angels' tongues are still,
And seraphs hush their golden strings,
In thy high presence, King of kings !

How then shall I, a clod of clay,
Or lift my voice, or tune my lay?
  Thou! who the realms of space and time
Dost people with thy might sublime,
Whose power is felt below, above,
  Felt in thy wisdom, in thy love;
Whose awful voice is heard around,
Heard in its silence as its sound;
Whose lovely spirit does pervade,
Alike the sunshine and the shade,
And shines and smiles in sorrow's night
As clearly as in pleasure's light.
  Lord! thou hast thunders—but they sleep;
Storms—but they now their prisons keep;
Nothing is breathing below, above,
But the spirit of harmony, joy, and love;
Nothing is seen or heard around,
But beauty's smiles, and music's sound,
Music re-echoed in earth and air:
Beauty that's visible every where,
Join the concert—share the joy;
Why should the cares of earth alloy,
Pleasures which Heaven itself has given,
Heavenly pleasures, which lead to heaven?

TRUST IN JESUS.

ANON.

WHEN, streaming from the eastern skies,
The morning light salutes my eyes,
O Sun of Righteousness divine !
On me with beams of mercy shine,
Chase the dark clouds of guilt away,
And turn my darkness into day.

When to heaven's great and glorious King
My morning sacrifice I bring ;
And, mourning o'er my guilt and shame,
Ask mercy in my Saviour's name ;
Then, JESUS, sprinkle with thy blood,
And be my Advocate with God.

As every day thy mercy spares
Will bring its trials and its cares,
O Saviour ! till my life shall end,
Be thou my counsellor and friend ;
Teach me thy precepts all divine
And be thy great example mine.

When pain transfixes every part,
And languor settles at the heart;
When, on my bed, diseased, opprest,
I turn, and sigh, and long for rest;
O great Physician! see my grief,
And grant thy servant sweet relief.

Should Poverty's consuming blow
Lay all my worldly comforts low,
And neither help nor hope appear,
My steps to guide, my heart to cheer;
Lord! pity and supply my need,
For thou, on earth, wast poor indeed.

Should Providence profusely pour
Its various blessings in my store,
O keep me from the ills that wait
On such a seeming prosperous state!
From hurtful passions set me free,
And humbly may I walk with thee.

When each day's scenes and labours close.
And wearied nature seeks repose,

O

With pard'ning mercy richly blest,
Guard me, my Saviour, while I rest;
And, as each morning sun shall rise,
O lead me onward to the skies!

And at my life's last setting sun,
My conflicts o'er, my labours done;
JESUS, thine heavenly radiance shed,
To cheer and bless my dying bed;
And from death's gloom my spirit raise
"To see thy face and sing thy praise."

THE CHRISTIAN PILGRIM.

ANON.

PILGRIM, burden'd with thy sin,
  Come the way to Zion's gate;
There, till mercy speaks within,
  Knock, and weep, and watch, and wait.
Knock—he knows the sinner's cry;
  Weep—he loves the mourner's tears:
Watch—for saving grace is nigh;
  Wait—till heavenly grace appears.

Hark, it is thy Saviour's voice!
  " Welcome, pilgrim, to thy rest!"
Now within the gate rejoice,
  Safe, and own'd, and bought, and blest.
Safe—from all the lures of vice;
  Own'd—by joys the contrite know;
Bought by love—and life the price;
  Blest—the mighty debt to owe!

Holy pilgrim! what for thee
  In a world like this remains?
From thy guarded breast shall flee
  Fear, and shame, and doubts, and pains.
Fear—the hope of heaven shall fly;
  Shame—from glory's view retire;
Doubt—in full belief shall die;
  Pain—in endless bliss expire.

SABBATH RETIREMENT.

EAST.

Here, in this solitude profound,
Pause, my soul, 'tis holy ground !
Come, lay thine earthly cares aside,
Jehovah whispers, " I'll provide."

Thrice welcome to this aching breast,
Long wearied in pursuit of rest ;
Thrice welcome is the lonely hour,
As the calm port when tempests lower.

O God, my God! alone with thee,
Here lock'd in holy secrecy,
All my guilt shall be disclosed,
All my wants on thee reposed.

Abhor me not—although I be
Abhorrible in all to thee.
Myself I loathe—myself I shun—
But seek a refuge in thy Son.

Redeeming love ! atoning blood !
I plunge into the cleansing flood :—
'Tis done ;—faith's simple act is done !
My soul-polluting guilt is gone.

Detested sin ! 1 hate thy name :
My Saviour's death ! my nature's shame !
The feet I pierc'd I bathe with tears,
While filial love supplants my fears.

Spirit of peace ! descend, and rest
A constant inmate in my breast ;
Calm the rough passions of my soul,
Constrained beneath thy mild control.

Still hover here, Celestial Dove !
Infusing faith, and hope, and love :
Nor let an earth-born care intrude
Upon my Sabbath solitude.

THE CHRISTIAN'S HOPE AND TRIUMPH.

CONDER.

WHO would not be a Christian? Who but
    now
Would share the Christian's triumph and his
    hope!
His triumph is begun. 'Tis his to hail,
Amid the chaos of a world convulsed,
A new creation rising. Mid the gloom
Which wraps the low concerns of states and
    kings,
He marks the morning star; sees the far
    East
Blush with the purple dawn: he hears a
    trump,
Louder than all the clarions and the clang
Of horrid war, swelling, and swelling still,
In lengthening notes, its all-awakening call—
The trump of jubilee. Are there not signs,
Thunders and voices, in the troubled air?
Do ye not see, upon the mountain tops,

Beacon to beacon answering? Who can
    tell
But all the harsh and dissonant sounds, which
    long
Have been—are still—disquieting the earth,
Are but the tuning of the varying parts
For the grand chorus, which shall usher in
The hastening triumph of the Prince of
    Peace!
Yes; his shall be the kingdoms. He shall
    come,
Ye scoffers at his tarrying! Hear ye not,
E'en now, the thunder of his wheels! Awake
Thou slumbering world! E'en now the
    symphonies
Of that blest song are floating through the
    air—
Peace, peace on earth, and glory be to God.

TIME MISIMPROVED.

MIDDLETON.

As o'er the past my memory strays,
  Why heaves the secret sigh ?
'Tis that I mourn departed days,
  Still unprepared to die.

The world, and worldly things beloved,
  My anxious thoughts employed ;
While time unhallowed, unimproved,
  Presents a fearful void.

Yet, holy Father, wild despair
  Chase from this labouring breast :
Thy grace it is which prompts the prayer
  That grace can do the rest.

My life's best remnant all be thine ;
  And when thy sure decree
Bids me this fleeting breath resign—
  Oh, speed my soul to thee !

WHAT IS TIME?

MARSDEN.

I ASK'D an aged man, a man of cares,
Wrinkled, and curv'd, and white with hoary
    hairs ;
" Time is the warp of life," he said, " O tell
The young, the fair, the gay, to weave it
    well !"

I ask'd the ancient venerable dead,
Sages who wrote, and warriors who bled:
From the cold grave a hollow murmur flow'd,
" Time sow'd the seeds we reap in this
    abode !"

I ask'd a dying sinner, ere the stroke
Of ruthless death life's " golden bowl had
    broke ;"
I ask'd him, What is time ? " Time," he
    replied,
" I've lost it, Ah, the treasure !" and he
    died !

I ask'd the golden sun and silver spheres,
Those bright chronometers of days and
    years;
They answer'd, "Time is but a meteor's
    glare,"
And bade me for Eternity prepare.

I ask'd the seasons, in their annual round
Which beautify, or desolate the ground;
And they replied (no oracle more wise,)
"'Tis folly's blank, and wisdom's highest
    prize!"

I ask'd a spirit lost, but, O the shriek
That pierced my soul! I shudder while I
    speak!
It cried, "a particle! a speck! a mite
Of endless years, duration infinite!"

Of things inanimate, my dial I
Consulted, and it made me this reply,
"Time is the season fair of living well,
The path to glory, or the path to Hell."

I ask'd my Bible, and methinks it said,
" Thine is the present hour, the past is fled ;
Live ! live to-day ! to-morrow never yet,
On any human being, rose or set!''

I ask'd old father Time himself at last ;
But in a moment he flew swiftly past ;
His chariot was a cloud, the viewless wind
His noiseless steeds, that left no trace behind.

I ask'd the mighty Angel, who shall stand
One foot on sea, and one on solid land ;
" By heav'ns, great King, I swear the mys-
      tery's o'er !
Time was,'' he cried,—'' but Time shall be
      no more !''

CHRIST A PRESENT HELP.

GRANT.

WHEN gathering clouds around I view,
And days are dark, and friends are few,
On Him I lean, who, not in vain,
Experienced every human pain.
He sees my griefs, allays my fears,
And counts and treasures up my tears.

If aught should tempt my soul to stray
From heav'nly wisdom's narrow way,
To fly the good I would pursue,
Or do the thing I would not do;
Still He, who felt temptation's power,
Shall guard me in that dangerous hour.

If wounded love my bosom swell,
Despis'd by those I priz'd too well;
He shall his pitying aid bestow,
Who felt on earth severer wo;
At once betray'd, denied, or fled,
By those who shared his daily bread.

When vexing thoughts within me rise,
And, sore dismay'd, my spirit dies;
Yet He who once vouchsafed to bear
The sick'ning anguish of despair,
Shall sweetly soothe, shall gently dry,
The throbbing heart, the streaming eye.

When, mourning, o'er some stone I bend,
Which covers all that was a friend,
And from his voice, his hand, his smile,
Divides me for a little while;
Thou, Saviour, mark'st the tears I shed,
For thou did'st weep o'er Lazarus dead.

And, oh, when I have safely past
Through every conflict but the last.
Still, still unchanging, watch beside
My painful bed—for thou hast died:
Then point to realms of cloudless day,
And wipe the latest tear away.

THE EMBLEMS OF DEATH.

BISHOP HORNE.

SEE the leaves around us falling,
  Dry and wither'd, to the ground;
Thus to thoughtless mortals calling,
  In a sad and solemn sound :—

Sons of Adam, (once in Eden,
  Where, like us, he blighted fell,)
Hear the lesson we are reading,
  Mark the awful truth we tell.

Youth on length of days presuming,
  Who the paths of pleasure tread,
View us, late in beauty blooming,
  Number'd now among the dead.

What though yet no losses grieve you,
  Gay with health and many a grace;
Let not cloudless skies deceive you;
  Summer gives to Autumn place.

Yearly in our course returning,
  Messengers of shortest stay,
Thus we preach this truth concerning,
  Heaven and earth shall pass away.

On the tree of life eternal,
  Oh let all our hopes be laid!
This alone, for ever vernal,
  Bears a leaf that shall not fade.

FRIENDSHIP.

POLLOK.

MANY sounds were sweet,
Most ravishing, and pleasant to the ear;
But sweeter none than voice of faithful friend,
Sweet always, sweetest heard in loudest
    storm.
Some I remember, and will ne'er forget,
My early friends, friends of my evil day;
Friends in my mirth, friends in my misery
    too;

Friends given by God in mercy and in love.
My counsellors, my comforters, and guides;
My joy in grief, my second grief in joy ;
Companions of my young desires ; in doubt
My oracles, my wings in high pursuit.
Oh, I remember, and will ne'er forget
Our meeting-spots, our chosen sacred hours :
Our burning words, that uttered all the soul ;
Our faces beaming with unearthly love;
Sorrow with sorrow sighing, hope with hope
Exulting, heart embracing heart entire.
As birds of social feather helping each
His fellow's flight, we soared into the skies,
And cast the clouds beneath our feet, and
  earth
With all her tardy leaden-footed cares,
And talked the speech, and ate the food of
  heaven.

TRUE HAPPINESS.

POLLOK.

TRUE happiness had no localities,
No tones provincial, no peculiar garb.
Where duty went, she went ; with justice
    went
And went with meekness, charity, and love.
Where'er a tear was dried ; a wounded heart
Bound up ; a bruised spirit with the dew
Of sympathy anointed ; or a pang
Of honest suffering soothed ; or injury,
Repeated oft, as oft by love forgiven.
Where'er an evil passion was subdued,
Or virtue's feeble embers fanned ; where'er
A sin was heartily abjured and left ;
Where'er a pious act was done, or breathed
A pious prayer, or wished a pious wish,—
There was a high and holy place—a spot
Of sacred light, a most religious fane,
Where happiness, descending sat and smiled.

P

CONFESSION.

ANON.

Lord, when we bend before thy throne,
  And our confessions pour,
Teach us to feel the sins we own,
  And shun what we deplore.

Our contrite spirits pitying see,
  And penitence impart;
And let a healing ray from thee
  Beam hope upon the heart.

When our responsive tongues essay
  Their grateful songs to raise;
Grant that our souls may join the lay,
  And rise to thee in praise.

When we disclose our wants in prayer,
  May we our wills resign;
And not a thought our bosom share,
  Which is not wholly thine.

Let faith each meek petition fill,
    And waft it to the skies;
And teach our hearts 'tis goodness still
    That grants it or denies.

FAREWELL.

BARTON.

NAY, shrink not from that word "Farewell!"
As if 'twere friendship's final knell;
    Such fears may prove but vain:
So changeful is Life's fleeting day,
Whene'er we sever—Hope may say
    We part, to meet again!

E'en the last parting earth can know,
Brings not unutterable wo,
    To souls that heavenward soar.
For humble Faith, with stedfast eye
Points to a brighter world on high,
Where hearts, that here at parting sigh,
    May meet—to part no more!

A PRAYER.

BOWDLER.

O God! my heart within me faints,
And pours in sighs her deep complaints;
Yet many a thought shall linger still
By Carmel's height and Tabor's rill,
The Olive Mount my Saviour trod,
The rocks that saw and own'd their God.

The morning-beam that wakes the skies,
Shall see my matin incense rise;
The evening seraphs, as they rove,
Shall catch the notes of joy and love;
And sullen night, with drowsy ear,
The still-repeated anthem hear.

My soul shall cry to thee, O Lord!
To thee, supreme incarnate Word!
My rock and fortress, shield and friend,
Creator, Saviour, source, and end!
And thou wilt hear thy servant's prayer,
Though death and darkness speak despair.

Ah! why, by passing clouds opprest,
Should vexing thoughts distract thy breast?
Turn, turn to Him, in every pain,
Whom never suppliant sought in vain;
Thy strength in joy's ecstatic day,
Thy hope when joy has passed!

A DOMESTIC SCENE.

HEMANS.

'Twas early day—and sunlight stream'd
  Soft through a quiet room,
That hush'd, but not forsaken seem'd—
  Still, but with nought of gloom;
For then, secure in happy age,
  Whose hope is from above,
A father commun'd with the page
  Of heaven's recorded love.

Pure fell the beam and meekly bright,
  On his grey holy hair,
And touch'd the book with tenderest light
  As if its shrine were there;

But oh! that patriarch's aspect shone
    With something lovelier far—
A radiance, all the Spirit's own,
    Caught not from sun or star.

Some word of life e'en then had met
    His calm benignant eye,
Some ancient promise, breathing yet
    Of immortality:
Some heart's deep language, when the glow
    Of quenchless faith survives,
For, every feature said—"I know
    That my Redeemer lives."

And silent stood his children by,
    Hushing their very breath,
Before the solemn sanctity
    Of thought, o'er-sweeping death:
Silent—yet did not each young breast
    With love and reverence melt?
Oh! blest be those fair girls—and blest
    That home where God is felt.

RACHEL.

PARK.

1 WILL not weep, my boy, for thee,—
Though thou wert all the world to me!
I would not wish thee wak'd again,
To strive like me with want and pain.
I will but close that still bright eye,
And kiss that brow so pale and high,
And those pure lips, whose tones divine
Caught their first words, first pray'rs from
      mine,
And fold thee to this bosom lone,
Which thou hast left as cold's thine own,—
And thus, implore the God who takes,—
To help the heart thine absence breaks!
My boy,—my boy,—this darken'd earth
   Shall never more to me seem fair;
And I shall stand, 'mid all its mirth,
   Like something which should not be there!

Yet 'twas to heav'n thy soul was borne,
And wherefore should thy parent mourn?
Perhaps in mercy, He reprov'd
The selfish zeal with which I lov'd.
I'll mourn no more! my God, thou know'
The wealth my desolate heart has lost!
Oh! shield me from repining cares,
When other parents point to theirs;
Bring back that light I now behold,—
Oh, these lov'd features,—calm and cold,-
That deathless smile, which whispers me
He died in peace and joy with Thee!
My boy,—my boy,—sustaining Pow'r
 Thy sinking mother well may crave,—
For welcome shall be that blest hour,
 Which sees her share thy lonely grave!

THE CRUCIFIXION.

CROLY.

CITY of God! Jerusalem,
  Why rushes out thy living stream?
The turban'd priest, the hoary seer,
  The Roman in his pride are there!
And thousands, tens of thousands, still
Cluster round Calvary's wild hill.

Still onward rolls the living tide,
  There rush the bridegroom and the bride;
Prince, beggar, soldier, pharisee,
  The old, the young, the bond, the free;
The nation's furious multitude,
All maddening with the cry of blood.

'Tis glorious morn;—from height to height
  Shoot the keen arrows of the light;
And glorious in their central shower,
  Palace of holiness and power;
The temple on Moriah's brow,
Looks a new risen sun below.

But woe to hill, and woe to vale!
　Against them shall come forth a wail:
And woe to bridegroom and to bride!
　For death shall on the whirlwind ride:
And woe to thee, resplendent shrine,
The sword is out for thee and thine.

Hide, hide thee in the heavens, thou sun,
　Before the deed of blood is done!
Upon that temple's haughty steep,
　Jerusalem's last angels weep;
They see destruction's funeral pall,
Black'ning o'er Sion's sacred wall.

Like tempests gathering on the shore,
　They hear the coming armies' roar:
They see in Sion's hall of state,
　The sign that maketh desolate—
The idol—standard—pagan spear,
The tomb, the flame, the massacre.

They see the vengeance fall; the chain,
   The long, long age of guilt and pain :
The exile's thousand desperate years,
    The more than groans, the more than
       tears ;
Jerusalem, a vanished name,
Its tribes earth's warning, scoff, and shame.

Still pours along the multitude,
   Still rends the heavens the shout of blood,
But on the murderer's furious van,
   Who totters on ?   A weary man;
A cross upon his shoulders bound—
His brow, his frame, one gushing wound.

And now he treads on Calvary,
   What slave upon that hill must die ?
What hand, what heart, in guilt embrued,
   Must be the mountain vulture's food ?
There stand two victims gaunt and bare,
Two culprit-emblems of despair.

Yet who the third? The yell of shame
　Is frenzied at the sufferer's name;
Hands clenched, teeth gnashing, vestures
　　torn,
　The curse, the taunt, the laugh of scorn,
All that the dying hour can sting,
Are round thee now, thou thorn-crowned
　　King!

Yet cursed and tortured, taunted, spurned,
　No wrath is for the wrath returned,
No vengeance flashes from the eye;
　The sufferer calmly waits to die:
The sceptre-reed, the thorny crown,
Wake on that pallid brow no frown.

At last the word of death is given,
　The form is bound, the nails are driven;
Now triumph, Scribe and Pharisee!
　Now Roman, bend the mocking knee!
The cross is reared. The deed is done.
There stands Messiah's earthly throne!

This was the earth's consummate hour;
  For this had blazed the Prophet's power;
For this had swept the conqueror's sword,
  Had ravaged, raised, cast down, restored;
Persepolis, Rome, Babylon,
For this ye sank, for this ye shone.

Yet things to which earth's brightest beam
  Were darkness—earth itself a dream.
Foreheads on which shall crowns be laid,
  Sublime, when sun and star shall fade,
Worlds upon worlds—eternal things—
Hung on thy anguish, King of kings!

Still from his lip no curse has come,
  His lofty eye has looked no doom;
No earthquake burst, no angel brand
  Crushes the black, blaspheming band.
What say those lips by anguish riven?
"God, be my murderers forgiven!"

He dies in whose high victory,
　The slayer, Death himself, shall die:
He dies! by whose all-conquering tread,
　Shall yet be crushed the serpent's head;
From his proud throne to darkness hurled,
The god and tempter of this world.

He dies, creation's awful Lord,
　Jehovah, Christ, Eternal Word!
To come in thunder from the skies;
　To bid the buried world arise;
The earth his footstool, heaven his throne!
Redeemer, may thy will be done!

LINES LEFT AT A REV. FRIEND'S HOUSE.

BURNS.

O THOU dread Power, who reign'st above!
　I know thou wilt me hear:
When, for this scene of peace and love,
　I make my prayer sincere.

The hoary sire—the mortal stroke,
   Long, long, be pleas'd to spare ;
To bless his little filial flock,
   And show what good men are.

She, who her lovely offspring eyes
   With tender hopes and fears,
Oh, bless her with a mother's joys,
   But spare a mother's tears !

Their hope, their stay, their darling youth,
   In manhood's dawning blush ;
Bless him, thou God of love and truth,
   Up to a parent's wish !

The beauteous, seraph, sister-band,
   With earnest tears, I pray,
Thou know'st the snares on every hand,
   Guide thou their steps alway.

When soon or late they reach that coast,
   O'er life's rough ocean driven,
May they rejoice, no wand'rer lost,
   A family in Heaven !

VENI CREATOR.

DRYDEN.

CREATOR Spirit, by whose aid
The world's foundations first were laid,
Come visit every humble mind ;
Come pour Thy joys on human kind ;
From sin and sorrow set us free,
And make Thy temples worthy Thee.

Oh, source of uncreated light,
The Father's promised Paraclete !
Thrice holy fount, thrice holy fire,
Our hearts with heavenly love inspire ;
Come, and Thy sacred unction bring,
To sanctify us, while we sing.

Plenteous of grace, descend from high,
Rich in Thy sevenfold energy ;
Thou strength of His Almighty hand,
Whose power doth heaven and earth command.

Proceeding Spirit, our defence,
Who doth the gift of tongues dispense,
And crown'st thy gift with eloquence.

Refine and purge our earthly parts;
But, oh, inflame and fire our hearts!
Our frailties help, our wills control,
Submit the senses to the soul:
And when rebellious they are grown,
Then lay Thy hand, and hold them down.

Chase from our minds the infernal foe,
And peace, the fruit of love, bestow;
And lest our feet should step astray,
Protect and guide us in the way.

Make us eternal truths receive,
And practise all that we believe:
Give us Thyself, that we may see
The Father, and the Son, by Thee.

Immortal honour, endless fame,
Attend the Almighty Father's name;
Q

The Saviour Son be glorified,
Who for lost man's redemption died ;
And equal adoration be,
Eternal Paraclete to Thee.

GOD VISIBLE IN HIS WORKS.

ANON.

ABOVE—below—where'er I gaze,
Thy guiding finger, Lord, I view.
Traced in the midnight planets' blaze,
Or glistening in the morning dew;
Whate'er is beautiful or fair,
Is but thine own reflection there.

I hear thee in the stormy wind,
That turns the ocean wave to foam ;
Nor less thy wondrous power I find,
When summer airs around me roam ;
The tempest and the calm declare
Thyself,—for thou art every where.

I find thee in the noon of night,
And read thy name in every star
That drinks its splendour from the light
That flows from mercy's beaming car :
Thy footstool, Lord, each starry gem
Composes—not thy diadem.

And when the radiant orb of light
Hath tipp'd the mountain tops with gold,
Smote with the blaze my weary sight
Shrinks from the wonders I behold :
That ray of glory bright and fair,
Is but thy living shadow there.

Thine is the silent noon of night,
The twilight, eve—the dewy morn ;
Whate'er is beautiful and bright,
Thine hands have fashioned to adorn :
Thy glory walks in every sphere,
And all things whisper, " God is here !"

A PRAYER TO JESUS.

HEBER.

When our heads are bow'd with woe,
When our bitter tears o'erflow;
When we mourn the lost, the dear,
Gracious Son of Mary hear!

Thou our throbbing flesh hast worn,
Thou our mortal griefs hast borne,
Thou hast shed the human tear;
Gracious Son of Mary, hear!

When the sullen death-bell tolls
For our own departed souls;
When our final doom is near,
Gracious Son of Mary, hear!

Thou hast bow'd the dying head;
Thou the blood of life hast shed;
Thou hast filled a mortal bier;
Gracious Son of Mary, hear!

When the heart is sad within,
With the thought of all its sin;
When the spirit shrinks with fear,
Gracious Son of Mary, hear!

Thou the shame, the grief, hast known,
Though the sins were not thine own,
Thou hast deign'd their load to bear,
Gracious Son of Mary, hear!

THE SABBATH ON THE SEAS.

GODWIN.

'TIS sweet to hear the Sabbath bells
Ring out on woodlands, floods, and fells;
Now clear and jubilant, anon,
Mellowed and mournful they chime on.
And sweet from church or chapel reared,
Midst glens, to rural hearts endeared,
Oh, sweetly, on the morning air,
Sounds the meek hymn ascending there,
When rural voices join to raise
An anthem to their Maker's praise!

And solemn and majestic floats,
The organ-chant in rolling notes,
Poured richly down the pillared aisle
Of some time-hallowed gothic pile.
When mingle then in prayer and song,
A city's thousand voices strong;
Oh, who unmoved can listen then
To the responsive deep Amen?
The soft refulgent light that streams
Through windows mapped with holiest
    themes;
The blazonry of the cherub wings,
Proclaim thy temple, King of kings!
And marbled tablets, sculptured round,
Mark where the dead have refuge found.

Such are the Sabbath-notes that rise
From earth's vast altar to the skies;
And have the ocean-waves no voice
To bid the sacred hours rejoice?
Have they, who on the dangerous deep
For life an anxious vigil keep,

No tribute for the Almighty One,
Who rules them from his viewless throne?
Hark! o'er the wide and bellowing main
Soft music comes, a choral strain.
And, kneeling on the barrier frail,
(How vain their strength if that should fail!
   That lifts them from the yawning sea,
Bold rugged men are grouped in prayer,
   In child-like pure simplicity,
And, lo! their God is with them there.

MARY MAGDALENE.
NOEL.

THERE is a tender sadness in that air,
While yet devotion lifts the soul above ;
Mournful though calm, as rainbow-glories
    prove
The parting storm, it marks the past despair!
Heedless of gazers, once with flowing hair
She dried his tear-besprinkled feet, whose
    love,

Powerful alike to pardon and reprove,
Took from her aching heart its load of care,
Thenceforth nor time nor pain could e'er
    efface
Her Saviour's pity; through all worldly scorn,
To her he had a glory and a grace,
Which made her humbly love and meekly
    mourn.
Till by his faithful care she reached the
    place—
Where his redeemed saints above all griefs
    are borne.

THE UNKNOWN GRAVE.

MOIR.

WHO sleeps below?—who sleeps below?
    It is a question idle all!
Ask of the breezes as they blow,
    Say, do they heed, or hear thy call?
They murmur in the trees around,
And mock thy voice—an empty sound!

A hundred summer-suns have shower'd
  Their fostering warmth, and radiance
    bright;
A hundred winter-storms have lower'd
  With piercing floods, and hues of night,
Since first the remnant of his race
  Did tenant this lone dwelling place.

Was he of high or low degree?
  Did grandeur smile upon his lot?
Or, born to dark obscurity,
  Dwelt he within some lowly cot,
And, from his youth to labour wed,
From toil-strung limbs wrung daily bread?

Say, died he ripe, and full of years,
  Bow'd down, and bent by hoary eld,
When sound was silence to his ears,
  And the dim eyeball sight withheld;
Like a ripe apple falling down,
Unshaken, 'mid the orchard brown:

When all the friends that blest his prime,
  Were vanish'd like a morning dream ;
Pluck'd one by one by spareless Time,
  And scatter'd in Oblivion's stream ;
Passing away all silently,
Like snow-flakes melting in the sea ?

Or, 'mid the summer of his years,
  When round him throng'd his children
    young,
When bright eyes gush'd with burning tears,
  And anguish dwelt on every tongue,
Was he cut off, and left behind
A widow'd wife, scarce half resign'd ?

Perhaps he perish'd for the faith—
  One of that persecuted band
Who suffer'd tortures, bonds, and death,
  To free from mental thrall the land,
And, toiling for the martyr's fame,
Espoused his fate, nor found a name !

Say, was he one to science blind,
  A groper in earth's dungeon dark?—
Or one, whose bold aspiring mind
  Did in the fair creation mark :
The Maker's hand, and kept his soul
Free from this grovelling world's control?

Hush, wild surmise!—'tis vain, 'tis vain,
  The summer-flowers in beauty blow,
And sighs the wind, and floods the rain,
  O'er some old bones that rot below;
No other record can we trace
Of fame or fortune, rank or race!

Then what is life, when thus we see
  No trace remains of life's career?—
Mortal! whoe'er thou art, for thee
  A moral lesson gloweth here;
Putt'st thou in aught of earth thy trust?
'Tis doom'd that dust shall mix with dust.

What doth it matter, then, if thus
  Without a stone, without a name
To impotently herald us,
  We float not on the breath of fame;
But, like the dewdrop from the flower,
Pass, after glittering for an hour;

Since soul decays not: freed from earth,
  And earthly coils, it bursts away;—
Receiving a celestial birth,
  And spurning off its bonds of clay,
It soars, and seeks another sphere,
And blooms through heaven's eternal year!

Do good: shun evil: live not thou
  As if at death thy being died;
Nor Error's syren voice allow
  To draw thy steps from truth aside;
Look to thy journey's end—the grave!
And trust in Him whose arm can save.

"THY KINGDOM COME."

CUNNINGHAM.

When my sad heart surveys the pain
Which weary pilgrims here sustain,
    As o'er the waste of life they roam!
Oppressed without, betrayed within,
Victims of violence and sin,
    Shall I not cry, "Thy kingdom come!"

And when I know whose strong control
Can calm and cheer each troubled soul,
    And lead these weary wanderers home
Can lodge them in a Father's breast,
And soothe this weary world to rest,
    Shall I not cry, "Thy kingdom come!"

O rise, the kingdom of the Lord!
Come to thy realms, immortal Word!
    Melt and subdue these hearts of stone;
Erect the throne which cannot move:
Stretch forth the sceptre of thy love,
    And make this rebel heart thine own.

WHERE IS GOD?

SHOBERL.

Where is He?—Ask his emblem,
  The glorious, glorious sun,
Who glads the round world with his beams
  Ere his day's long course is run.
Where is He?—Ask the stars that keep
  Their nightly watch on high.
Where is He?—Ask the pearly dews,
  The tear-drops of the sky.

Where is He?—Ask the secret founts
  That feed the boundless deep;
The dire simoom, or the soft night breeze
  That lulls the earth to sleep.
Where is He?—Ask the storm of fire
  That bursts from Ætna's womb;
And ask the glowing lava flood
  That makes the land a tomb.

Where is He?—Ask the Maelstroom's whirl,
  Shivering tall pines like glass;
Ask the giant oak, the graceful flower,
  Or the simplest blade of grass.
Where is He?—Ask behemoth,
  Who drinketh rivers dry;
The ocean-king, leviathan,
  Or the scarce-seen atom fly.

Where is He?—Ask the awful calm
  On mountain-tops that rests;
And the bounding, thund'ring avalanche
  Rent from their rugged crests.
Ask the wide-wasting hurricane,
  Careering in its might;
The thunder-crash, the lightning-blaze,
  Earth all convulsed with fright.

Where is He?—Ask the crystal isles
  On arctic seas that sail;
Or ask, from lands of balm and spice,
  The perfume-breathing gale,

Where in the universe is found
  That presence-favour'd spot;
All, all, proclaim His dwelling-place,
  But say—Where is He not?

THE END.

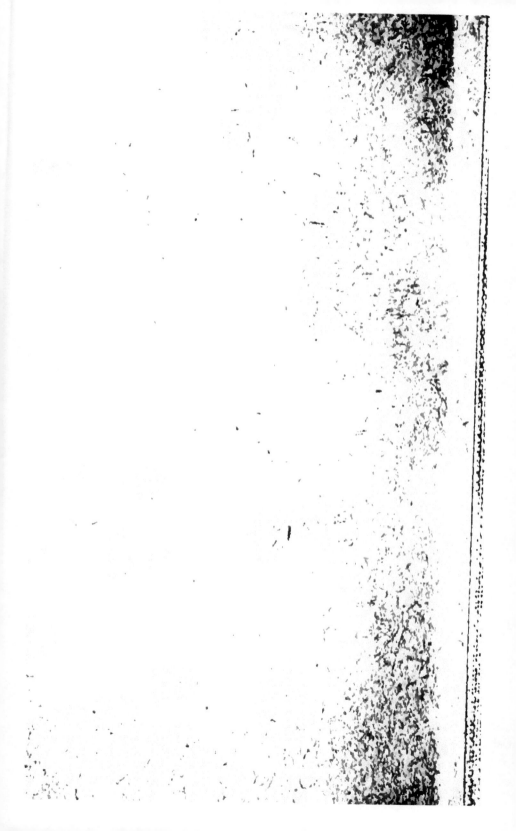

ImTheStory.com

Personalized Classic Books in many genre's

Unique gift for kids, partners, friends, colleagues

Customize:

- Character Names
- Upload your own front/back cover images (optional)
- Inscribe a personal message/dedication on the inside page (optional)

Customize many titles Including

- Alice in Wonderland
- Romeo and Juliet
- The Wizard of Oz
- A Christmas Carol
- Dracula
- Dr. Jekyll & Mr. Hyde
- And more...